ABOUT THE TITLE

In Hawai'i there was no written language until the white people began to settle there in the mid-1800s. The way knowledge was transmitted, whether history or cultural values or skills for daily tasks, was by storytelling. Beginning with the Hawai'ian story of Creation, it was learned word for word from elders to young people, just repeating the story aloud.

When written language developed, in many places in the world, usually only a very few "learned" people learned to read and write. Most people still were illiterate, and learned history and cultural values, as well as the recent news, from storytelling. It is only in the last three generations that it has become common in the world for most people to be able to read!

Living in Hawai'i, I was charmed by the custom of saying to a friend one encountered by chance, "Let's get together and talk story." It meant we would just plan to meet to tell each other what we had been doing and thinking about. Or remembering. But I loved the phrase, "Talk Story."

As we grow older, much of our thinking is taken up by remembering. So when I was collecting my little accounts of various memories from my 90 years of living, I thought that this term would be good to use in the title for my book.

I hope you will read just one story at a time. I hope you will read it aloud, even if you are alone.

Now here we are together. Let's talk story.

LET'S
TALK STORY

For Eloise,

It's good to share
our stories,
Beth Gawain

by

Beth Gawain

Short Stories From
My Long Life

    Let's Talk Story/Beth Gawain – 1st ed.
ISBN-10: 1511524499
ISBN-13: 978-1511524490
    1. Short Stories   2. Memoir

CONTENTS

DEDICATION

This book is lovingly dedicated to two dear Ones:

To my beloved daughter, Shakti Gawain, for urging me to write, to believe that my memories are of value, and for supporting me in every way to go ahead and do this book.

And to my very dear "daughter- sister- friend," Jessica Fleming. Ever since we met, in a hot tub with three other friends, in New Zealand in 1982, she has taken care of me as her beloved elder. She has loved me unfailingly. She has always seen me, and encouraged me to be, my best self. Thank you always Jessica.

~ 1 ~
BIG DECISION

The conference had lasted all day, trying to determine new policies. No one had agreed with anyone else's good ideas. Back in my office in the HUD building in Washington, DC, I was standing at my desk in front of my big leather chair, looking out my window. It was a delectable view out over the spread of autumn's pallet. Having this office, with this view, was a privilege accorded me as recognition of my years of achievement. My career as a city and regional planner had always been interesting, often clogged with controversy, but certainly never dull. But how many, many, many hours more am I going to endure in the model of this day? I had spent my career trying to get some important person to be aware of how <u>his</u> fine solution to <u>his</u> problem was going to impact some other problem. I was always trying to get everything to work together more smoothly.

It was 1974. I was 53 years old … (big sigh).

I began to think of the recent death of my mother. Her life had been very different from mine. For her generation, it had been what she wanted: a wife, mother of a boy and a girl, homemaker in a nice house, a leader of cultural events in our town. Then much had been lost in the depression, so that, from my first job, part of every paycheck had gone to my mother. Now that need was gone.

My daughter had graduated from college, and had spent two years travelling around the world with friends. Now she was established and supporting herself. I had always saved, and had invested prudently. For some time now I had lived comfortably. I had no wish to live extravagantly. A couple of years before, I had begun to practice yoga, and had found whole new experiences in exploring different levels of mind. I had toyed with the idea of going to India to explore that further.

As I stood at my desk, looking out my window, remembering this day of discussions, the thought of trying to resolve it all into something useful became increasingly distasteful. Well ... my mother and my daughter don't need my paycheck any more ... what if ... what if ....

It was a faint whisper in my ear, ..."You don't have to do this anymore"....

Then it hit me like a physical blow on the chest:

"YOU DON'T HAVE TO DO THIS ANYMORE!"

I fell back into the big chair behind me.

I'll never forget that moment of realization, how the glorious feeling rushed through me.

I was <u>free</u>! I could just quit. I could go anywhere in the world. Do anything. Be anything.

I could be free of schedules, not required to do some particular duty every hour of every day.

I could live <u>spontaneously</u>. Imagine.

I took a few deep breaths and looked all around me. The handsome desk and chairs and bookcases, the fine pictures and colorful charts, the exotic potted palm in the elegant ceramic pot. Do I need any of this any more? I felt quite detached from <u>everything</u>.

I got up and headed purposefully out my door. As I passed my secretary's desk she held up a cluster of pink message slips, "You have ..."

"I'll be right back," I said, and headed down the hall to the office of the personnel director for our division. I told the clerk in the outer office that I wanted the form that I would submit to quit.

She looked at me. "I beg your pardon. What did you say?" She knew who I was. I did realize that my request would be a surprise.

I smiled. "I just want to submit a request to quit."

Quite flustered, she got up and went to the open door of the inner office. The director came out, and I repeated my statement.

She looked at me blankly for a moment, then said, "Please come in here," motioning for me to enter. I went in and she closed the door behind me.

"Now tell me what has happened."

I smiled. "No, no. There hasn't been any kind of incident."

"Are you not getting appropriate assignments?" It was a common problem in the 70s for professional women to be given assignments that were not commensurate with their ability.

"No, no. Dick is a good boss. He gives me real responsibility, lets me do it my way, is available to discuss anything I come to him with. No, everyone here treats me with friendly respect. It's nothing like that. I just want to quit working."

She had pulled my folder out of her file for a quick glance. Then she studied me. "You're not old enough to retire."

"Yes, that's right. I'm not talking about retiring. I mean to quit working."

"You'd get no pension at all until you're 55. And then all the rest of your life you'd get a much smaller pension than if you work to 55."

"Yes, I realize that."

After assuring herself that my health was all right, and that I wasn't getting married, she said, "Only two more years, and you'd collect full retirement all the rest of your life. It's a big difference. Anyone could work two more years at something. You're really good at your job."

" I'm sorry. I just want to stop working."

Finally she found the correct form. I was about to sit down right there and fill it out. "No, you take it home and think it all over carefully. Talk it over with someone. It's a very big decision."

So I did.

I never wavered. She got the form the next day.

That's how I quit my job. Ended my career. And went to India.

~ 2 ~
SEE THE PRETTY ROSEBUDS

Recently a group of us were remembering the fashions of the 1920s, when we were small children. I recalled the beautiful dress my mother wore to go dancing at the country club. I was not quite three years old. My mother had always sewn her own attractive clothes, but this was a very special "ready-made" dress, an unusual treat. When she wore it she looked elegant. And because it was shorter and had flounces, she also looked playful, which was unusual for my mother.

It was yellow chiffon, and was embroidered all over with little red rose buds, about eight inches apart. Mother warned me not to touch it: my hands were often grubby. But she draped the skirt over my face several times so I could feel how soft it was. It hung on a hanger with her other clothes in her closet. We both loved it.

I was an extremely shy child. Whenever anyone that I didn't know well came to the house, I would go hide in a closet, while Townsend, my confident four-year-old brother, went to charm them in the living room.

One such day (strangers in the living room), I crawled into my mother's closet, leaving the door a little open, so I wouldn't be in the dark. There on the floor, under the hanging clothes, was my mother's mending basket.

Remember what a "workbasket" was? Housewives never used to sit around with idle hands. If they weren't crocheting or tatting or knitting, they were probably darning socks as they talked. The workbasket held a pin cushion with pins and needles, a thimble, spools of various colored thread, a little box of buttons, a card of snaps and a card of hooks-and-eyes (this was long before zippers were invented). There were several socks with holes waiting to be darned. The small scissors were enchanting. They were shaped like a golden stork, with the moving blades forming its beak, and the stork's head, body and feet forming the rest of the scissors.

I was not usually allowed to handle those scissors. But now ... here they were. Just the right size for my little hand. Sitting here on the floor of the closet, what could I find to cut? No paper here, among the shoes and other things around me.

Then the soft chiffon of the special dress fell against my face. Here were the pretty little rose buds. Maybe I could cut one out ... and hold it in my hand? I had been praised for how well I could cut out printed red hearts for valentines.

(Dear reader, I'm sure you have guessed the rest of this story. This tragedy.)

I tried cutting carefully around one little rose bud, and sure enough, there it was, all my own, in my little hand. I tried another one. I was surprised at how skillful I was at just cutting right around each small bud, without taking much of the surrounding cloth. Soon I had a collection of wonderful rose buds that I could play with.

Then I heard my mother calling and coming to find me. I was so proud for her to see how carefully I had been able to use the scissors. I came out of the closet with my treasures in my hand to show her.

But no! When she saw what I was holding, she drew a great gasp, as her hand flew to her mouth. She pulled out the hanger with the beloved dress, and saw all the holes that

I had cut from the very front of the skirt. She looked back at my startled face. Clearly, I had not intended any harm.

My mother sank into a chair, the ruined dress in her lap, and she cried and cried and cried. As, of course, did I.

She never punished me for it. But I have never forgotten it.

How innocently we can cause great distress to someone else, when we had not meant to do any harm at all.

~ 3 ~
WHAT'S RUDE

In my years of travel around in many countries in the world, there were two things that I found the most interesting. One was how astoundingly gorgeous is our planet earth.

The second most interesting to me is how very different are the myriad cultures of the world. One detail I noticed over and over was what kind of personal behavior is considered to be rude in any particular culture. And how arbitrary are those judgments!

For example, in America, to see someone put her finger up into her nostril and dig around ... well, we feel an involuntary shock. (When a small child does that, the mother pulls his hand away, and the child learns that is "not done.") In some other parts of the world, I noticed, the finger in the nose is commonly done in polite society, and causes not a ripple of notice.

When I was living in an ashram in India, the old ladies who lived there were scolding me almost every day for some outrageously rude thing I had done, just because I didn't know it was "rude." For example:

One evening three of them converged on me as we were leaving the meeting hall, after listening for an hour to a revered swami. They were scolding me for disrespect.

"What did I do?" "You pointed your feet at the Swami!" "I did <u>what</u>?"

We had all been sitting on the floor, which they had always done. There were no chairs in the room. A 4-folded blanket, used as a cushion, was the classic way to seat oneself, with feet tucked under. I was 54 years old, and I had spent most of my life sitting in chairs. It was painful for me to sit on my feet for long periods of time. So that evening I had shifted my legs briefly, a couple of times, to have them straight out in front of me for a few minutes. Since I was facing the speaker ... well ... I <u>had</u> "pointed my feet at the Swami," a really rude gesture. I learned to shift my feet to one side when I couldn't bear it any longer. I truly did not want to be disrespectful.

In America, it is considered rude to <u>stare</u> at someone. If we catch a glimpse of a person who has a deformity, we look away. If someone is just <u>behaving</u> oddly, we may sneak a peek from behind the menu, or we may take off a jacket in order to twist far enough to get a better look. We don't just openly stare.

I remember an example. We were having dinner in a fine restaurant. A new party of three were ushered to the next table: a tall man, an elegant lady, and a tall boy of maybe seventeen. When the man turned to face my direction as he sat down, I saw that it was <u>Gregory Peck</u>! In my very personal estimation, Gregory Peck is absolutely the most beautiful man that ever lived. And here he is at the next table, out for an evening with his wife and son. My whole body can feel the magnet pulling my eyes to his direction. I simply must not, MUST NOT, stare at him.

My own companion was happily surprised at the unusually pointed attention he received from me during that dinner. I am proud to say that I did succeed in <u>not</u> staring at that fabulously attractive man at the next table.

It is a really important courtesy in our culture.

In much of Asia, staring is not a behavior that is of any concern. To them, if something is unusual, or just interesting, you naturally <u>look at it</u>.

As I travelled around in India, Sri Lanka, Nepal, Indonesia, Malaysia and Thailand, often, I myself was a sight that was uncommon for most people to see. So naturally, they looked at me. "Here is this unusually tall, older woman, travelling alone. Her skin is very pale, and her hair and eyes are light brown. She wears our clothing, but she doesn't get it quite right. Isn't that interesting to see." They did stare at me.

I never stayed in tourist hotels, or travelled first-class. It was much cheaper, and more interesting, to use the accommodations used by the Asians themselves, and to travel on second-class buses and trains. I was a more uncommon sight among those local populations. And yes, they did stare.

There were many children everywhere I went, and they, especially, were drawn to gather around and just watch me. Often I would try to get them to show me something, about their clothing, or their environment. But sometimes I just got tired of having no privacy to relax.

I remember once in the mountains of Thailand, near the end of my second year in Asia, I was travelling on a second-class bus, in an area of no foreign tourists at all. The bus stopped for a tea break, and everyone got off. I wanted to stretch and relax, and found a large stone, off to one side, where I sat down with my cup of tea. No sooner had I settled than a ring of village children formed, about four feet around me. I so needed to relax, after being so long on the crowded bus!

Their manner was the least bit tentative, as if they were not quite sure it was safe to be near me. That gave me an idea for how I might be rid of them.

I glared at them. I raised my arms, and shouted, "BOO!!"

They scattered in terror, and were gone! I was able to relax....

It was a few weeks later that I flew from Singapore to Sydney, Australia. I slept on the plane, and felt truly transported when I arrived. I walked into the crowds of people in the busy airport. Nearly all were pale-skinned people, speaking English.

I walked through the airport with a real spring in my step. I noticed that I was feeling wonderfully free, and easy, and buoyant. Lighthearted. I wondered why I had this unusual sense of great freedom.

Then I realized:

No one was staring at me.

I looked just like everyone else.

~ 4 ~
I ALMOST DIED IN KABUL

No, it wasn't in the recent times of war in Afghanistan. It was in 1975. Nor was it caused by any violence. It was a fairly common scenario for American travelers in that part of the world: I had dysentery. And I had not taken it seriously enough.

From the first few months of this trip, when I had traveled around southern India and Sri Lanka, I had had occasional bouts of diarrhea. I had dropped a noticeable amount of weight. I was always careful about boiling the water, and about drinking water only from my own canteen that I carried. At the roadside tea shops, I drank tea only if poured directly from the boiling tea-kettle, and I ate fresh fruit only if I could peel it myself. The served meals of grains and beans and vegetables were always thoroughly cooked into mush and served from the steaming cook pot. Nevertheless, at times I would get diarrhea. Then I would just fast. I would eat nothing for a day or two, sleep a lot, and drink plenty of boiled water. In a few days, I'd be all right.

I had spent three months in a yoga ashram with 300 devotees, nearly all of them people of India, with only about a dozen of us European or American. Then I traveled around the Himalayas for some time before spending two months in Buddhist meditation at 8,000 ft. with a group of young people from Australia, Canada and Scandinavia. During all this time I had increasingly frequent and severe episodes of dysentery. Always I just fasted, and rested. And got better. I was in such an exalted frame of mind that it never occurred to me to be concerned about my health. Everybody among us had dysentery at times.

After nearly a year, I started to travel back toward California where my daughter was living. I took a flight from New Delhi to Kabul, intending to spend a week on tours to the various glorious old mosques around Afghanistan, then to proceed overland to England.

On the plane my seatmate was Al. He was a tall blue-eyed mid-west American man, probably under 40, who was serving as a leader of the Peace Corps Volunteers in Afghanistan, who were mostly in their 20s. (I had just recently ended my career as a city planner. At 54, I was in a yet "older generation.") He gave me advice about finding good tours out of Kabul. When we landed, his wife, Dee, was there to meet him, and we chatted, waiting for the baggage. She was a friendly, intellectual young black woman from Central America.

Al gave me their phone number. "Don't hesitate to call us if you need anything."

I checked into the cheap 'hippie' hotel that had been recommended by other world-wanderers I'd met in India. It was truly basic, but very clean. Shared toilets and washing facilities were across the hall, telephone down at the end of the hall.

I hadn't eaten for two days, because I was in one of my episodes. Totally exhausted, I crawled between the clean sheets, and fell asleep. And slept ... And slept ...

I would rouse from my sleep, have a sip of water, notice that it was dark outside the window; sleep again; rouse again, to drink and notice that it was light. Sleepily, I thought I should be making arrangements and going on my tours, but sleep would again overcome me ...

22

When it was dark again, I began to have vague thoughts that this was not just sleep ... I was passing out ... Was that OK? ... I could just never wake up ... It was blissful, really. Just floating ... Very few thoughts ... Lightness of being ... Floating in bliss ...

It was daylight again. I could just reach the canteen to wet my mouth. I roused enough to be sure to close the canteen again without spilling, and to realize that that was important.

Should I make an effort? ... To do what? ... I drifted off again. Then I became conscious enough to think about where I am. I'm in this little old hotel in Afghanistan. I could just die here. My daughter doesn't even know where I am. When I thought about that, I did come more into consciousness.

If I just floated away ... out of life ... and my daughter was told that her mother's body had been found in this shabby little hotel in Afghanistan ... no, it couldn't happen that way ... I began to feel that I must DO something ...

I tried to rouse myself enough to think. What could I do? How could I come out of this?

I needed help. Who could help me? Where was there any help?

I had to try to THINK. I'm in this strange country alone ... Then I remembered the Peace Corps couple who gave me their phone number ... My little address book ... it's in the outer pocket of my big backpack ... There is the backpack, right there. Can I get myself out of bed to reach it? It seems a monumental effort ...

Yes, I did it. I then crawled on my hands and knees down the hall to the telephone. I managed to place the call.

Dee answered right away. I told her my name. "Do you remember me?"

"Yes. Are you alright?" (I guess it was obvious that I was NOT all right.) I said, "No."

"Where are you?" I was able to tell her the name of the hotel. "I'll be right there."

Later she told me that she came and found me collapsed on the hall floor by the telephone.

I don't remember any of this, but Dee took me to the Peace Corps doctor, who immediately diagnosed amoebic dysentery. He dosed me with amoeba poison to kill the amoebas in my gut.

Dee and Al took me kindly into their home. Dee cleaned me up, installed me in their guest-room bed, and began to fill me with fluids. As I became more and more aware, I knew how incredibly lucky I was! Their cook was a local man who made the most delicious soups. At first they were thin liquid, but soon became more and more substantial, and utterly delectable.

They kept me for two weeks. They had a little girl and a baby boy, and two servants. Dee had a fine collection of American literature, so I spent many long hours reading well-written stories, and loved talking with her about them. Al liked American popular music, and was a good drummer. He would put on a record, sit at his trap set, and enthusiastically bang away, while we sang along. I could play peek-a-boo with the baby, and board games with the charming little girl.

At regular intervals all day we heard the call to prayer from a nearby mosque. The deep-toned melodic rhythms became a part of my return to living. Dee told me that the

words at dawn are saying, "Prayer is better than sleep."
Yes. It's good to wake up ... to be alive.

From the window I could see down into the
neighborhood, to a street crossing. There were few
motorized vehicles in this time of 1975. There were
pushcarts and pedestrians, mostly men. The women were
usually wearing the black garment that completely covered
them from head to toe. Dee wore ordinary American skirts
and jackets, and I saw occasionally a woman dressed that
way, not attracting unusual attention. She said that it was
widely accepted for women to dress as she did, but that
many women preferred to be covered. Dee did have one of
those black garments.

"Would you like to try it on?" I did. As she draped it
over me, I felt claustrophobic. There was a little pill-box
cap from which fell the long full drapery all the way to the
feet, with only slits where the hands could reach out. A
small strip of black lace allowed the eyes to see. It was hard
to imagine walking around with so little view of the
surroundings. I noticed that, on the street, the men were
respectful of the fully covered women, deferring to them at
the street crossing, and stepping aside for them to pass. I
did remember in my early childhood when men had been as
polite as that to women in my Texas town!

After two weeks, I was gaining strength. When the
Peace Corps doctor had weighed me, earlier, although I
was 5'8" tall, I had weighed only 110 lbs. When I rallied to
120 lbs., I began to be able to walk fairly briskly. When I
finally could put on the backpack and walk around, it was
time to go.

One day I made a little outing to downtown Kabul to arrange to go overland to Teheran, and on to Istanbul. At a local silversmith, I bought Dee a silver-and-lapis bracelet.

Next day, I left.

I never saw them again.

~ 5 ~
WHERE OH WHERE CAN IT BE?

Now in my nineties, I am in an assisted-living community where a frequent refrain is, "Where can it be? I had it right here!" The "it" involved can be the spoon, or the scarf, the reading glasses, the cell phone, or even the wallet. But commonly it will be the keys. My keychain is easy to identify because it includes a handcrafted silver heart. I had discovered this delightful artifact 40 years ago, as I was admiring the fine silver crafts in the Mediterranean island of Sardinia. At the time, a popular song was "I Left My heart in San Francisco," but to everyone who admired my silver heart, I warbled, "I found my heart in Sardinia." It has graced my varying clusters of keys all these years, making it possible for me to say with certainty, "Yes, those keys are mine." I particularly remember one occasion when the beguiling silver heart played a crucial role for me.

I had been car-camping around Western Australia for three months in the 1980s. I had another month on my passport visa, and decided to drive along the whole south coast, ultimately to reach Sydney on the east. Ahead of me was surely one of the most unpopulated places in the world. It is about a thousand miles across the Nularbor Plain. "Nul arbor" meaning "no tree." (And, by the way, no people!) All that coastline is very high cliffs, straight down deep into the ocean. As I started my 2-day drive along this Great Australian Bight, I knew I was leaving the last beaches before the great cliffs began. I decided to stop for a last beach swim.

I turned off on a dirt road toward the ocean. The sign said Cape Arid Weather Station. "Cape Arid." OK, I get it.

No vegetation, only great sand dunes stretching southward, forming the Cape. There was a small building with some tall metal structures holding weather-gauging equipment. No cars in the 4-slot parking lot. No answer to my knock on the door. The only movement was the desultory turning of the wind gauge. Well no, as always in Australia, there were scurrying lizards. Then a noisy flock of colorful lorikeets passed overhead.

I locked my little campervan. With only a big hat and a small day-pack, I set off on the path beside the high dunes of powdery white sand. Gaps between the dunes revealed an appealing beach on the other side, so I chose one gap and trudged over. (It didn't occur to me to notice which gap I came through!)

A long firm beach stretched ahead, sloping into gradually deepening ocean with gently breaking waves. High tides had left a line of seaweed and flotsam far along the beach. Maybe some shell treasures to find? No people at all. Glorious! My light sandals go easily into the backpack so I can wriggle my toes in the cool damp sand.

I stroll along, poking into the detritus, stopping to enjoy being all alone in this glorious world. Only peeping pipers to notice me. Blue, blue sky and sea, with white ruffles at water's edge making splashy sounds. Enough breeze to cool my skin from the full morning heat of the sun. Yes, glorious. Suddenly there is a splash out there in the ocean, then another. Dolphins! What fun. The land is indeed desolate and lifeless on Cape Arid, but the sea and sky are full of life. A swarm of minnows are swishing through the shallows, pursued by bigger fish. Then three of the local red-legged gulls come swooping along and chase the fish out deeper. Soon there are numbers of gulls fluttering and plunging. A squabble begins as they compete for the fish, and the squawking and splashing attract even more gulls.

Dolphins farther ahead are also finding fish, diving, surfacing with a live fish, then neatly swallowing it whole. I have done much dolphin-watching, and have never seen dolphins compete for a fish. Their manner with each other is more: "Oh, is that one yours? OK, this is mine. Life is bountiful." Overhead is a splendid scene: a V-formation of Australian great white pelicans. They fly in perfect rhythm with each other, and perfect V form, as they pass on westward. A wave washes near and releases a crab, which scurries up the beach and into its hole.

Out in the really deep water there is a whoosh sound, and I see the vapor from a whale's breath, as it empties its huge lungs, and instantly refills them with air. I watch and see its tail lift as it dives again into the depths. This is the Indian Ocean home of the leviathan known as the Right Whale. I feel privileged to be in its presence. I sit down on the beach to let myself take in how lucky I am to be here.

It's easy to peel off my few clothes and run splashing into the ocean. Lovely and cool floating there. I always appreciate that the salt water is holding me up, so unlike sinking into a freshwater pool. The saltwater buoys me. Mother Ocean is supporting me, sustaining me. I am her beloved child. All life began in the water. I am totally relaxed and at peace, one with the universe, floating in endlessness.

Finally back out, I am quickly dry and dressed, and eating the juicy mango I had brought. The wind is picking up. I am glad it is behind me as I walk back, making footprints beside the faint ones I had made in the opposite direction. No one but me and the birds and the waves to imprint the beach. No, there are some crab holes. I admire the patterns created by sand pellets that the crabs throw out as they dig deeper.

OK, where is the place where I came through the dunes? My faint footprints show where I turned. Good. As I trudge through the deep soft sand , my feet are sinking in. I'm glad to get past the dunes and see my van in its parking place. Tracks show there has been another car, but it's gone now. I reach into my pocket for my keys.

They are not there …

Not in the other pocket, either. Feeling around in the back-pack … no keys. I dump the few things out of the pack, and search carefully … no keys. I clearly remember locking the car with the key, so I know it's not locked inside the car. Where, oh where can it be?

What will I do? I look carefully all around the car. No keys.

No one around for help. I try the door of the building. There's no one there. I look back toward all that sand. The wind has become strong, and sand is blowing everywhere. If I dropped the keys out there, by now they could be completely covered. And I had walked a long way on the beach. They could be anywhere.

I remember a brain-training class where we practiced finding something hidden. Now is the time for using that practice.

I quiet my mind. Then I imagine seeing the keys, and I focus on the vision of the keys on their chain. There are the keys on their chain, there is the beloved silver heart, very vividly. Now I am supposed to imagine looking around it, to see its surroundings…. Well it's laying on the sand, but it's the damp bare sand down at the beach. There are clusters of seaweed, and wave marks from receded tides. Oh good. At least they seem not to be in the dunes. I head back through the gap, hoping it's true that the keys are not in this deep soft dry sand. I'd never find them.

I'm vague about how far I had gone along the beach. The clusters of seaweed all look alike. The training was that I should keep the mind fixed on the vision of the object, and trust my intuition to guide me. I've become fairly good at being aware of my intuition.

I find some of my footprints, but most are faint. It seems most likely that the keys would have dropped at the place where I took off my clothes. How FAR was that? It has been some distance now since I've seen my old footprints.

Ah, up there ahead, I had made more of a disturbance of the surface where I left my things and went into the water. Hope arises. I'm scanning eagerly as I approach. I don't see anything but ruffled sand. I look all around. Where, oh where …

Finally, I sit down, feeling really deeply disturbed. What will I DO if I really can't find my keys? I bury my face in my hands and allow myself to fully feel despair and desolation. I am really all alone out here.

Eventually, I try to THINK. An agitated anxious mind is not a good problem-solver.

A little voice inside tells me, "You've lost touch with your intuition."

Yes. I settle down.

I take a long DEEP breath. I straighten up and look out to sea, and bring back the memory of feeling so glorious here in this spot. The white gulls are still soaring in the blue sky. The curve of a seagull's wings, as the bird glides, may be the most perfect curve shape of any in all creation. And I am privileged to see it now.

Calmly, I again visualize the keys, and the shining silver heart, and find my deep inner confidence. It will be all right, whatever happens. Whatever happens, it will all work out.

I have been feeling the wind as an antagonist. Now I will perceive it as my friend, blowing at my back as I return along the beach. I get up and glance all around me. Even though there is nothing there, I feel good. Grace and ease are my natural state. I pick up my things, and start back.

And then stop.

There. Something bright. Something shiny, almost covered by the blowing sand. My dear, dear silver heart catching the sunlight! Here are my keys.

The lost is found! My Sardinian heart.

~~~~~

So! I've written my story for this week. Time for lunch. Where is the folder that I use, to take my story to class. I had it right here. Maybe I put it back in the cupboard. No, it's not there.

Where, Oh Where Can It Be?

QUAKER BONNET

Sorting through the storage locker, we find one box that is particularly familiar. I remove some tissue paper and show my daughter what is nestled inside.

I ask her, "Do you remember this?" She lifts out the object made of fine grey straw and grey ribbons.

" It's our ancestor's little Quaker bonnet! Of course I remember." I was pleased that she went on, "At the big family gathering, we took photographs of each of the female cousins trying it on. We all looked very proper," she recalled. "And we looked pretty. It's actually flattering to wear, isn't it." That's true. It is a becoming style. "Wasn't her name Elizabeth?"

I tell her, "Yes, she was Elizabeth Betterton Turner, mother of my grandfather, on the eastern shore of Maryland."

We took the little box home, and now, here it is in my closet, in my elder community. At lunch, I tell my other 90-year-old table companions the story.

My great-grandfather, Richard Townsend Turner, was part of a Quaker community on the shore of Chesapeake Bay in the mid-1800s. His wife, Elizabeth Betterton, was known as a beauty, and a capable manager of household and servants. She also was of course as devoted to Quaker values and principles as was he.

Richard Turner built a dock and created an enterprise of shipping the local farm products up the Chesapeake, through the Delaware River to Philadelphia. Like other Quakers, he was known to be scrupulously fair and trustworthy in his business, and he made a good success. A little town began to form around the dock, and Mr. Turner named the community "Betterton," in honor of his wife's Quaker family, who had been among the earliest settlers there.

While I was living in Washington D.C., in 1970, my niece and I went to visit the town of Betterton. There is a dock there with a little amusement park and some food shops. We found the little Quaker cemetery with gravestones for Richard and Elizabeth and for three of their offspring. No trace of the meeting-house, nor of the Quaker school, where two of my eldest aunts had gone to first and second grades in the 1890s. We also found the house where they had stayed with their grandparents, that same Richard and Elizabeth.

We knocked on the door, and the owners were pleased to have us look around. In the dining room, I remembered one story my aunt used to tell:

"The little girls were required to practice good table manners. After they finished eating, they had to stay at the table, for at least five more minutes of table conversation, before they could ask to be excused. From their chairs they could see the big grandfather clock in the entry hall, to count the minutes for their release. We were told this story when we were little, and eager to go play. Now I see exactly where the clock would have been." I felt a wave of nostalgia as I pictured my beloved aunts, as children sitting there.

We were shown the kitchen, now completely modernized. "Up here were the slave quarters," they gestured up the back stairs.

"Oh. No," I said, "they didn't have slaves. They were Quakers, and they were ardent abolitionists. There would have been servants living here, and they would have been black people, but they would have been freed people."

"Oh, how interesting. There are still some Quakers around Betterton, but we didn't realize our house had been involved." That led me to tell them how their house had been really involved.

"The Turner shipping business took the local farm products from Maryland to Pennsylvania, so of course, that is across the Mason and Dixon Line. When the produce was loaded by black men on my great-grandfather's dock, he didn't pay close attention to counting how many of those men were his neighbors' slaves, and how many of those had come off the boat before it sailed away. He himself hired free men, white or black, to work for him, and they were paid a living wage.

"One local farmer or another began occasionally to come up short of a slave, after they had sent a shipment of produce to Philadelphia. They began to be more watchful of which three or four of their slaves had gone down to the dock to carry the heavy loads, and to make sure they all had returned to the farm! After a month or so, they might become more lax, and another slave might be missing. Of course a slave was valuable 'property.'

"They held a meeting, and confronted Mr. Turner. He told them that his own employees were permitted to ride on the boat. For some of them, of course it was their job, to man the boat. He didn't feel an obligation to watch whether some slave involved in loading cargo might choose to stow away. (And get off in Philadelphia. And be free.)

"The neighboring farmers didn't think that attitude was very neighborly. They came one night with torches, to tar-and-feather him!

35

The story has been handed down through the generations, of his lady's faith.

"Elizabeth Betterton Turner went out on the veranda. She began to address the angry men in her quiet but confident Quaker manner. They gradually abated their menacing words and gestures. Somehow she appealed to their better natures.

"And in the end … they put down their torches, and they went away.

"End of story."

I have heard this story all my life. It was even written in a family history published in the early 1930s. And found in the Kent County history museum. I myself have worn her little grey bonnet. I have stood on the same veranda, looking down over the space where the men had been gathered. I could imagine the tension.

How sure of her faith she was, that human nature is based in good-ness! How sure she was that she could appeal to that better nature in those angry men, so that they lowered their torches, and turned away, and left!

But … what did she say???

No one kept any record of her words to them. We will never know what she said.

~ 7 ~
MEANT TO BE?

"Those letters will have to be burned," my mother said. When I looked startled, she explained, "When a girl marries, any letters she had received from other boys must be destroyed." I was about to be married. It was 1941. Mother's edict seemed old-fashioned to me, but not a big issue. Anyway, there certainly wasn't anything scandalous in any of those missives. As I looked through, I found only one letter that I hesitated to burn. That was because it was sort of an historic document.

It had been written to me in 1939 by Mahmoud Sipahi. He was a young man from Turkey, who, in June, had just completed his Master's degree at the U. of Wisconsin. I met him when I went there to summer school. I needed a few extra credits at the U. of Illinois, and had heard that Madison's lakeside campus was nicer in the summertime. It was, indeed.

I am often drawn to people from cultures different from mine. I like learning that there are different ways to view, and to deal with, issues of everyday life. Anyway, in addition to being from an exotic culture, Mahmoud was an attractive person, with warm dark eyes. He dressed and behaved like any American grad student, and was very fluent in English, with only the slightest accent. (He found my Texas accent charming!) He said he was soon returning to Turkey; so as we began to spend time together, I often asked him about differences in ways of life in Turkey.

I was very interested in what I learned. Attaturk, the "benevolent dictator," had brought Turkey into the modern world in the 1920s, diminishing the role of religion,

37

abolishing the wearing of the fez for men and the veil for women, and vastly increasing the role of women in public life. The girls that Mahmoud had met in America had not cared to hear about Turkey, so he was pleased to talk with me. He was to go in mid-August to New York, to board a ship for home, leaving America, perhaps forever. Travel in the 1930s was expensive and arduous.

One moonlit night in late July we were sitting on a lakeside dock, and I said, "Talk to me in Turkish." He was hesitant. "Why?"

"I just want to hear how it sounds. Talk about anything," I laughed, "I won't know what you're saying." He held my hand and looked out over the lake silently for a time. Then he began to speak, slowly and hesitantly. He had a pleasant voice anyway, but this was deeper and almost melodic, as he went on. He ended, and we both were looking out over the water.

I said, "That was beautiful. Was it poetry?" Still looking out, he said rather shortly, "Yes. It was poetry." Then silence. But I felt his emotion. Maybe he really missed using his own language. I felt, even though we were side-to-side-touching, and he held my hand warmly, that he had at some level drawn away from me. Then I realized that, at some other level, we were more intimate than we had ever been. It seemed that neither of us wanted to break away.

Finally he turned to me and took both my hands, looking deep into my eyes in the dim light.

"I want you to come to Turkey." I was silent, deeply touched but overwhelmed. "I want you to live with me and be married."

"Oh, Mahmoud!" was all I could say, but I squeezed his hands and laid my cheek to his.

I was completely flooded with unfamiliar, unexpected emotions. After a long moment he drew away and stood up, pulling me with him, and we walked away with his arm around me. "I can't take you with me now. And I know you need to think it all over, and talk with your family."

At the door of my dorm, he embraced me gently, kissed me tenderly, and left.

I was afloat.

During that last week in Madison, I took exams, and he was packing up the life he had had in America. We did see each other, and he talked earnestly about how Americanized our life would be in Istanbul, and how his family would welcome me. He was happily going into his father's import/export business, and we would live very comfortably. They had turned Christian many years earlier, but were not very religious; nor was I, at that time. I became caught up in the plans, without ever really saying, "Yes, I would marry him." (He didn't seem to even notice that detail!)

I was only 18 years old. I had come to Wisconsin still half in love with Jack, who had graduated from U. of Illinois in June. When we had parted we had both felt that it was a friendly ending, and I had heard from him only once all summer. But was I ready to be planning to marry someone else?

I took the train to Houston, where my mother and two brothers were living, to spend the six weeks before I would be heading back to Illinois for the fall semester. My family didn't take it very seriously when I told them about this man who wanted me to marry him and go to live in Turkey. Then the telegram came from Mahmoud, as he was sailing out of New York: "WILL BE BACK ONE DAY TO TAKE YOU." How romantic, everyone agreed. Was it meant to be?

So ... Dear readers, what world event occurred the end of summer, 1939? ...

Hitler bombed Warsaw, invaded Poland. England and France declared war on Germany. Within days all Europe was caught up in war. Would America be involved? My half-brother Franklin was already 30 years old, but my brother Townsend was just 20. He would be subject to the draft.

What would become of Mahmoud??? My heart was in panic. He was voyaging across the Atlantic. How would Turkey be involved? (In that era, ship's passengers were out of communication.)

In Sept. I had just gone back to college when my mother forwarded the letter. (The very letter I was later reluctant to burn.) Mahmoud had taken an Italian ship out of N.Y., to debark in Italy, and to go by land to Turkey. On the voyage he had begun a letter to me, writing a bit each day. Then one entry said: "Last night we sailed past Gibraltar with the ship's lights blacked out. They will not tell us passengers why. We cannot receive any news. We know there must be some big trouble in Europe. I am not sure what will happen to us when we reach port in Italy. I fear that Germany (which is friends with Italy) has made trouble with England (which runs Gibraltar) My Turkey is friends with England and America, so the Italians may prevent me from proceeding. If you receive this letter, you will know that I have been allowed to get on the train in Italy and leave."

I did receive the letter, so he did go on home to Istanbul! How awful, for the world to be in such turmoil.

I wrote to him, but he didn't receive the letter for weeks. He did write me from Istanbul, but our exchanges of letters took months. Each of us had too much happening, drawing us apart.

By a year later the connection was lost…. It seemed not meant to be.

Many, many years later, I was in Istanbul, for two days. At 54 years old, I was returning overland from my year in India. I loved seeing San Sophia, and the Bosporus, and having a bath in the grand old stained-glass-and-marble Turkish Bath.

On the street I did pass the thriving Sipahi Import-Export business. No, I did not inquire if Mahmoud was still alive. He would have been 60 years old. I felt no need to see a Mahmoud grown fat and bald, and surrounded by progeny.

Back in 1941, I had married, and I had indeed burned all the letters from former "admirers," as my mother described them. I am glad I do remember that telegram, and that one letter written in that historic week of 1939.

And I do remember a moonlit night of delicate emotions between a very young woman and an ardent young man. It is a delightful memory, for a very old lady now to treasure.

~ 8 ~
A "BAD" NEIGHBORHOOD?

As a new resident of Washington D.C. I wanted to join a Unitarian Church, which I had done when I lived in Sacramento. There was an old established Unitarian Church within a moderate driving distance from where I was living in Southwest D.C. I began to go there to Sunday services, and found it quite suitable.

It was 1968, and Washington was experiencing the throes of drug problems, combined with the race relations and poverty that were so troubling at that time. The church was in a neighborhood increasingly inhabited by poorer black people. Being Unitarian, the church was trying to welcome these residents into the congregation. The fairly new minister was a black man, but one who had considerably more educational and cultural advantages than did many of his neighbors. Already perhaps one-fourth of the congregation was black people, but they tended to be the more intellectually inclined. The church services and activities really did not appeal to the average residents of the neighborhood by 1970.

When I mentioned to my co-workers in my Federal office that I was going to that particular church, I was usually warned that it was in a "bad" neighborhood.

"Lots of drug problems. Be careful." We talked about the new methadone program that was being started, intended to help heroin addicts.

Well, Sunday morning seemed to me to be a fairly safe time of the week. I went regularly to the services for more than a year, and felt satisfied with my choice.

One Sunday morning I am a bit late leaving home. I drive into the vicinity of the church after services have already started, so no one is lingering out on the church steps, or in the portico. I park across the street, and I can hear the choir singing inside. As I get out of the car I put on my overcoat, and put my keys in the pocket. Then I hang my handbag on my arm and step out across the street.

I haven't seen that there is a black youth lurking between two cars parked on the church side of the street. As I head for the church entrance, he leaps out beside me and strikes me very hard on my back. He spins me around, and I see the blackjack in his hand. I see the desperate look on his face.

When he grabs my handbag, I start to cry out, and he hits me on the mouth. I fall down in a heap. He runs off with my purse.

I am conscious, but stunned, mouth bleeding, lying on the sidewalk.

There are two neighborhood boys across the street who have seen it all. They come running over to help me up. They give me a big kerchief to hold to my bleeding mouth.

I am confused and shocked.. Not only am I in pain, I can't even speak clearly, because my upper teeth are interfering with my tongue.

"Can you drive?" I manage to ask the larger boy. I find my keys in my coat pocket. They help me back into my own car, then drive me to an Emergency Room a few blocks away.

These two boys, 16 or 17 years old, heard the doctor say that the bone under my upper lip was broken and the teeth caved in. He said he could straighten all that;

however, one tooth was <u>gone</u>. They heard him say, "It's too bad we don't have that tooth. I could put it back in there, and it would probably stay."

So guess what they did.

Those boys walked back to the church. They found the tooth on the bloody sidewalk. They returned to the doctor, who was still stitching me up. He pushed the tooth into its space, and fastened it there. (It stayed for another 20 years.)

I was very shaken by all this.

Everyone was kind and helpful: the people in the E.R., the police, the friend from my apartment house who came to take me home, and kept me fed and coddled for a few days, my colleagues at work who took turns dropping in with well-wishes and reassurances, and food, and books.

I stayed in my fifth-floor apartment for two weeks as my mouth began healing. I would look out over the streets, wondering ... was I going to be uneasy just to walk around out there? ... maybe forever? Would I nervously imagine that a villain was lurking behind every pillar or post, to leap out and hurt me?

No, that didn't happen.

On my first walk back to work, I felt perfectly at ease with all those strangers hurrying along with their own concerns. I have since travelled the world with far less anxiety for safety than most people tend to have!

I'm sure that a big reason that I wasn't more traumatized was because of those two boys who immediately helped me.

I've had long thoughts about the three boys of that neighborhood. There were the two that were so wonderfully helpful. And there was the violent one. I never learned any of their names. The minister and I tried to find the helpful ones, but we never did succeed.

The police that day did recover my handbag (minus any cash) in a nearby alley. They never were able to identify the youth who attacked me. I still remember the desperation I saw in his face as he hit me. The police thought he was probably on drugs, and craving his fix. The purse didn't have enough cash to buy him even one dose.

The three boys wouldn't have seemed very different from each other. All were black, all dressed in long-worn clothes, all products of the same neighborhood.

One was headed down a road that would probably lead him to ruin.

The other two boys had already developed a very different approach to life. Even in the same neighborhood they must have found quite different influences. They had known different role models.

So was it a "bad" neighborhood?

I like to think, all these years later, that now the two boys are grandfathers. Now they are still demonstrating to the neighborhood how much happiness life can bring when we practice co-operation and kindness.

They are still helping to make it a "good" neighborhood.

~ 9 ~
THE LONGEST MAHOGANY BAR
IN THE CARIBBEAN

The Villa Olga was an old mansion on the island of St. Thomas, Virgin Islands. It was said to have been the Russian embassy more than 100 years earlier, back in the glory days of the Caribbean. When I went there, in 1951, the Villa Olga had been turned into a hotel, with a fine restaurant, and a saloon boasting to have "The Longest Mahogany Bar in the Caribbean." It certainly seemed an endlessly long stretch of gorgeous mahogany, very highly polished. One could imagine the variety of elbows that had polished it, wearing the many different kinds of sleeves of all the different fashions of the different eras and cultures of the fascinating individuals who had occupied this longest row of stools.

Upstairs there were four or five spacious bedrooms for tourists. Three little cottages were pleasantly scattered out on the extensive grounds. These were rented by the month.

With my two-and- a-half year old daughter, Carol Louise, I settled into one of these cottages. The plan was to stay the six weeks that the Virgin Islands required in order to establish residency. Then I would get a divorce. In the USA at that time, getting a divorce required accusing each other of terrible things. In the Virgin Islands we needed only to say, "We don't want to do this marriage any more." So that is the reason that I was on my first adventure to a tropical island.

The grounds of the Villa Olga had large spreading mahogany trees shading the lawns, as well as coconut palms, flame trees, and frangipani trees with their clusters of heavy-scented yellow blossoms. Everywhere there were tropical plants of varying sizes and colors. And there was balmy fragrant air. Ahhhhh. How glorious to be lightly clothed and to be truly warm, all the time.

We took a stroll around, and visited with Mark, the friendly proprietor. He seemed interested in the novelty of having a blonde little child staying at his place. Resting back at our cottage, I could see people walking along the far side of the property to go to the saloon to eat and/or drink. I would be making our meals in the kitchen of our cottage.

I had never been very interested in visiting bars. Rather than lose my sensibility in alcohol, I preferred to find bliss in birdsong, discover delight in sculpture, or chortle to a turn of phrase in literature. The Longest Mahogany Bar in the Caribbean held no attraction for me.

I took my little girl for a walk to the town along a shady road. The small wooden tin-roofed houses had banana trees and mango or papaya trees, in little yards crammed with tropical color and fragrances unfamiliar to me. There were also smells of cooking that were new to me, so that the sensory assault was stunningly agreeable.

There were very few vehicles. People ambled around everywhere in an easy and cheerful manner. One man was carrying a large basket full of bananas balanced on his head! I had heard that it was customary here to carry things that way. This made me notice what beautiful posture and grace of movement everyone displayed.

Carol pulled on my arm. "Mommy. Why are all the people chocolate?"

"Oh! Well, you remember our friend Joyce, whose skin was dark like this." After a thoughtful pause she nodded. I said, "In this part of the world most of the people are black. In the whole world more of the people have dark skin than are light-skinned like we are." ("Chocolate people," I thought. That's nice. And we are not really "white." We are more "vanilla," aren't we?)

Everywhere we went there was Calypso music, from radios mostly. Windows and doors were always open. I saw one woman doing her ironing, while her feet and hips were following the music. It was the beat of life in the Caribbean.

Next day we found the fine-sand beach. The clear water of the bay was unbelievably blue. We tested the warm caresses of the little waves. It became our ritual to walk along the detritus-strewn edge of the beach to see which washed-up seashells might be fresh and unbroken that day. Carol learned to say "little limpet" and could pick out that kind of shell.

The Villa Olga employees enjoyed my bright-eyed little girl. The gardener, the cook, the chambermaid, the bookkeeper, all greeted her when they encountered her. By the time we had been there a week, she was already picking up the Calypso cadence of their speech. She had easily adjusted to the concept that people could be any skin color.

It seemed that our life on St. Thomas had smoothly begun. But on only the third day, guess what? Little Carol came down with the chickenpox!

It turned out to be a very light case of chickenpox, She felt sick for only two days, and had very little rash. But the local doctor, very professional (and very chocolate), was concerned that she should not go where there were other children ... which was everywhere in St. Thomas! So we were confined to the grounds of the Villa Olga. I would settle down on the verandah of our cottage to read or write, and watch little Carol chase the lizards or the birds, and play with her own toys. Few people ever came near, except the employees, in passing.

Then one day there was a Navy vessel in the port. I could see groups of white-clad sailors going past on the far side of the grounds, heading for the Longest Mahogany Bar in the Caribbean.

I had been out Calypso dancing the night before, and I began to nod off in my too comfortable chair. When I startled awake ... where was she??? Nowhere in sight! Where would she go? Maybe over to see Mark. He'd be very busy. I hurried over to the saloon, and went in the big open door.

The Longest Row of stools at the Longest Bar—well, every stool was occupied by a white-clad sailor except for the one right in the middle. On that stool was a tiny yellow-dressed figure. She was sucking the straw of a lemonade, happily the center of attention of all those homesick American boys.

I went to fetch her. "You know, I told you that you need to stay away from people as long as you have spots, so they won't get sick too." I took her down from her stool and explained to the entranced young men that she had chickenpox, showing the few red spots on her neck and arms. As we went out the door, they all waved and called out, "Goodbye, Carol!" With a few wolf-whistles for me. (This was long before Women's Lib.)

An hour later, Carol was quietly absorbed with paper and crayons on the verandah when I went into the kitchen to get her supper. When I brought it out to her … uh-oh! My "baby" was losing her need to be near her mommy all the time. I took a few deep breaths. A little caution would be in order. But I must be very careful never to teach her to be <u>afraid.</u>

This time I knew where to look, and sure enough, there was another row of white-clad sailors, with one small yellow-clad figure on the middle stool. Another whole bunch of sailor-boys were exposed to chickenpox.

It happened that, for later that evening, I had been set up for a dinner date with an officer from the ship. After some conversation, I mentioned to him that my small child had chickenpox, and unfortunately had mingled with some of his sailors that afternoon at the Longest Mahogany Bar in the Caribbean.

He laughed. "Well that would be interesting. I'm glad you told me, because we would be wondering how in the world they caught it. Shall I write you if we have an outbreak of chickenpox?"

Sure enough, in due time I had a letter from him. Not only did his ship have a chickenpox episode, a number of the men had been transferred right away to other ships, and had taken the pox with them. He wrote, "Anyone in the Navy who hadn't had it as a child is finding chickenpox in the Navy."

It all originated at The Longest Mahogany Bar in the Caribbean.

~ 10 ~
THE GORILLA

At a conference about saving animals I met Fred and Judith, an older couple who enjoyed using their considerable wealth as patrons of the zoo. For a number of years they had been occasionally donating some particular animal that the zoo wanted to acquire. Then they were allowed to come visit 'their' animal to see how it was adapting to its zoo home. They invited me to come with them to see the young gorilla they had recently added to the zoo's already established gorilla tribe.

As a longtime observer of dolphins, I was interested in other highly intelligent animals. I had had three memorable encounters with elephants, so now I was eager to experience a gorilla, a different intelligent being.

My new friends arranged, with the zookeeper in charge of the apes, for us to come after the zoo was closed to the public one day.

The gorillas were kept in a large heavily fenced enclosure with a building in the center. The different animals had access to the building, each through it's own door, giving it a way to reach it's own shelter any time it wanted. Inside the building, the keepers used barred passageways to reach all the cages, in order to feed and care for the animals, where the public never saw them. This is where we were privileged to go.

The head gorilla keeper was Kate, a 40-ish woman of strong (!) stature and cheerfully confident manner, who welcomed me with a hearty handshake. She led the three of us at leisurely pace through the barred corridors, explaining as she went. Judith and Fred had been here often and knew which turn to take to visit their donated animal.

Kate stopped once to tell me, "This is the place for our big male, our silver-back. He's outside just now, but maybe he'll come in while we're here."

"Oh yes, I'd like to see him up closer! " He had looked very impressive outside, from some 50 feet away.

"We've had him nine years," she told me, "and he was barely mature when we got him. He has taken leadership of the whole group quite naturally, and they all accept and respect him with no trouble."

We went on to see the new young gorilla. When Judith and Fred went into the cage with Kate, I wasn't included, as was quite proper. After watching for a while, I told them, "I want to go back to see if the big male has come into his cage," and Kate said, "Sure, go ahead."

I went back around the corner to the big fellow's cage.

And there he was! I was more startled than he seemed to be. He continued concentrating on something on the floor back there, while I took a minute to adjust to being that close. He was about ten feet beyond the heavy steel bars of the cage, and I was about five feet on my side. Never had I imagined being in the close presence of such a BIG STRONG creature! Clearly it was no novelty to him to have a person standing by his cage, and I felt my startled caution easing away.

He glanced toward me a couple of times, and then slowly came over. He stood up, grasping the bars, and looked directly into my face.

He was not much taller than I am, but SO BIG! The sense of POWER was dramatic. But it was with so much ease! I found I did not feel threatened at all. Impressed, certainly, but not threatened. In fact, I felt drawn to him, and took a step forward, then quickly caught myself. Well … the bars were close enough together that those huge arms couldn't reach through …

There was coarse black hair on the arms and body and head, but I was surprised to see that the face was not bare skin: it had short thick fur, looking like soft black velvet. I longed to touch it. Imagine stroking that lustrous black velvet on the cheeks. He moved his face right up to the bars. And I moved closer, too. He looked softly right into my eyes. We exchanged the most deep and unguarded look, into each other's inner being. I was filled with lightness and grace.

I looked again at the huge fingers grasping the bars. Without another thought I barely touched a giant finger … and then stepped back.

He moved back too, and looked down at his finger. Then he brought his finger right up to his face … and smelled the place where I had touched it.

It had been an intense moment of inter-species intimacy.

Now it's my deeply treasured memory.

~ 11 ~
BICYCLE DAY

"Today I'm taking Barbara out to rent bikes and ride around Walden Pond. Would you like to join us? We're carpooling with some other graduate students, and there's room for you." It was a beautiful early October day in 1943, wartime. I was 22 years old.

"Oh yes. How nice of you. I'd love to come." I was new in Boston, working in a research lab at MIT, my brief marriage to a Navy husband having recently ended in divorce. The man on the phone, Norman, was an MIT grad student whom I'd run into here on the campus. We'd known each other when we were both undergraduates at University of Illinois. Here in Boston I'd met almost no one except my co-workers, and the three young women at the boardinghouse where I was living. Some social life would be very welcome.

I joined the group as they were ready to get into the three cars. Norman introduced me to Ted, who handed me into the back seat of his car, with two other people, and we were off.

It was grand to get out into the colorful autumn countryside. Everyone worked a 48-hour week in those days, so I'd had no time or energy to explore beyond the historic parts of downtown Boston. This was a real treat.

"There it is," said Ted, as we came into view of the water, "the famous Walden Pond."

"How absolutely delightful. We couldn't have picked a better day," we all agreed. The maple and oak trees were in full startling color. We parked at the bike rental place, and everyone piled out and began to decide which bike was the right size for which legs.

Ted found one that was different: a tandem bicycle (for two people). He pulled it out and rolled it over toward us.

"Look at this!" Several of us were looking. "Wouldn't it be fun to ride the bicycle-built-for-two? I've never done it but..." He looked straight into my eyes and said, "Who wants to try it with me?"

(It was the moment that changed my life.)

He was tall and handsome, with an ingratiating smile, an MIT grad student. How could I resist? Off we went, somewhat wobbly at first, but quickly mastering the balance, of the two bodies on one bicycle, and the balance of the male\female energy.

I've never known a comparable day. The warm sun caressed the grateful skin. The glorious blaze of autumn leaves was doubled by their reflections in the Pond. The sky was the vivid blue of a crisp autumn day, contrasting with the intensity of the reds and yellows and oranges of the foliage. Color almost always makes me happy, and I was very ready for cheering up. My body was pleased with the activity of pumping the bicycle and breathing in the country air, and pleased to be near an attractive male body that seemed eager to be near my female one.

We talked a little about Walden, and Thoreau. We exchanged "who-are-you's," about background and current activity. He was in his second of three years toward his doctorate in mechanical engineering, deferred from the draft because of being nearsighted. (The military didn't take men who wore glasses.) He was from a little mining town in Pennsylvania, where his father had emigrated at age 16 from Poland. So dad was a coal miner, who had sired three brilliant sons, Ted the eldest, who were being educated on full scholarships. Ted said they were a close family.

My childhood was also in a small town, but otherwise quite different. I was the youngest child, with two older brothers. My father owned the only shoe store in our Texas county of cotton farmers. My mother was the well-educated daughter of a Maryland doctor, and she was involved in cultural events in our community. It was never a solid marriage. The Depression broke my father, who just drove away one day and disappeared, when I was 13. My mother's wealthy relatives supported us, and sent us to college. My older brother had graduated from Rice and was doing well in Houston. Now, the brother next older to me was going into the Air Corps. Ted did already know, from Norman, that I was divorced.

We pedaled along easily. Neither of us was really athletic, but we'd grown up with bicycles as transport, and the track was smooth and even. On the tandem bike, my handles didn't steer at all, they were just to hold me steady, as Ted did all the steering up front. We both pedaled, but either of us could coast and the other keep going. We coordinated very naturally. The others were all ahead of us, so we didn't stop anywhere.

When we reached the bike return, there was a proposal to go to a nearby farmhouse that was famous for English-style afternoon tea. Norman caught my hand. "Barbara and I and some others have to go back to town, but you look like you're having a good time." He waggled his eyebrows. "Do you want to stay?"

"Oh yes!" Ted stepped in, taking my other hand. "I'll be glad to take her back to her place."

So we went to the charming white-clapboard country house fronted by big bright maple trees, where we had tea and crumpets. We were: lanky Mel, a fast-talker from the Bronx, said to be a genius in math; dark-eyed, blonde-haired, sparkly little Dora from Boston; big, redhaired, self-contained Frank, a Montana farm boy doing a doctorate in biology; and small droll Eduardo, from Bogota, Colombia, doing physics.

The mood was light. The rollicking witticisms, flying between those exceptional brains, sometimes were so intricate that I would take too long grasping one, and I'd miss the next one! It was an entertaining and delightful afternoon for me, getting to know my new "very close" friend, and seeing him interact with his buddies. When we headed back to the city, Frank and Eduardo were planning to have dinner at a Chinese restaurant on Mass. Ave. near where I lived. "Want to join them?" Ted asked me.

So for the first time in my life, I had Chinese food. They insisted we needed no forks on the table. I had no concept of the use of chopsticks. But I was very hungry, and … well … more adventure! By this time Ted was holding my other hand under the table.

When we finished, Eduardo said, in his intriguing accent, "Is young, the night. Is time for music, no?" He and some others had rented one of the big old brownstone mansions on Beacon St., just around the corner, and there was a grand piano. So we went there.

I then discovered yet another pleasure: The one who played the piano was Ted. (Eduardo told me that Ted's piano teacher, back in high school, had wanted Ted to have a career as a concert pianist.) I settled back into the soft divan. When was this dream going to end? He played Chopin. He played Rachmaninoff. He played Brahms. And he played marvelously.

It was late when, finally, with Frank still in the car, I made Ted let me out at the door of my boarding house, and I went in.

Would he call? He had taken my phone number. Surely he would. You never really knew, did you?

(He did call ...)

Of course, not for a moment had we realized, when we were pedaling a tandem bike down that sunlit autumn track at Walden Pond that we were riding off into our future together.

~ 12 ~
INVOCATION TO PELE – GODDESS OF FIRE

When I was living on Maui, I became involved in a co-op art group, working with clay for both pottery and sculpture. As we grew in numbers we needed a bigger kiln. So we built one ourselves, and decided to have a celebration to initiate using it. I wrote this invocation to the Hawaiian goddess, Pele, known to most tourists as the Goddess of the Volcanoes. She is prominent in Hawaiian culture as being very powerful and seductive. You want to keep on the good side of Pele, because she can be devastatingly destructive. We were about to use our new kiln to fire our clay creations. It's wise to appeal to Pele for support when you plan to use fire.

E Pele E
O Pele, glorious Pele, beauteous Pele,
Pele of the flaming hair,
Turn your blazing eyes to us here.

See this work of our hands
This kiln
This altar we dedicate to you, O Pele,
Creator of flames.
Make this kiln your altar,
O splendorous Pele.
Bring your sacred fire here,
O wondrous Pele.

See these earthen shapes we have made,
See these works of our hands,
Works of our spirits.

We offer them to you, O Pele,
Here on your very own altar.
Accept them as our joyful offerings to you,
O magical Pele.

Heat them with your intense fire,
Burn them brightly.
Keep the fire even and fine.
Heat these objects to their perfect glow,
Make their colors blazing and bright,
Or softly blending,
O glorious Pele, sacred Pele, powerful Pele.

Pele of the flaming tresses,
Pele of the burning eyes,
Behold these clay pieces
We now place in your altar.
Accept them
As our hearts' offerings to you.

Kiss them with your hot breath,
Caress them with your fiery fingers,
Work your own pure magic on them,
That when we shall open the kiln
You will amaze us
With the glories you have wrought
From our humble offerings,
O Pele.

Powerful Pele, fiery Pele,
Magical Pele, glorious Pele,
Pele of the sacred flames.

E PELE E.

A TEXAS FOURTH OF JULY IN 1927

Waking at the first faint light of dawn on the family
sleeping porch, Townsend (just eight) and I (age six) signal
each other to be quiet. Mother is a very light sleeper. It is
notable that we sneak out of our beds into the house, get
dressed in cotton shorts and shirts (bare feet are standard in
July), and gather the firecrackers and matches, without
alerting her. We are out the front door and down the
sidewalk to the street. While he is breaking open the bunch
of tiny one-inch firecrackers, I take out a match. The whole
neighborhood is still silent.

Townsend strikes the match and lights the fuse,
throwing the string of little firecrackers out onto the
pavement. POP POP POP pop-pop-pop-pop-pop-pop. We
did it! The first kids in the neighborhood to start the
fireworks on the Fourth of July! WE ARE THE FIRST!

Very quickly, down the block, the Mitchell boys have
theirs going, then Dan and Mary Ellen across the street.
Then the Leonards on the corner. Within a few minutes we
hear fireworks going off all over the south part of
Gainesville. WE WERE FIRST! (We never ever managed
it another year.)

The kids on our block gather at the one vacant lot, to
light more firecrackers. The older boys are daring each
other ("I double-dog dare ya!") to light a big fat 3-inch one
and hold it until just before it explodes, tossing it away in
the nick of time. I'm glad Townsend doesn't feel the need
to join in this challenge. We all know of a boy who lost a
finger, and another who lost an eye, that stupid way. For us,
just making noise, and more and more noise, is fun. After

dark tonight will be the glorious colored fireworks: roman candles and pinwheels. For morning all we need is NOISE.

Breakfast for each of us is half an orange, a bowl of oatmeal with raisins, and a glass of milk. [*It is straight from a cow out on the edge of town, delivered in a milk can to our kitchen door and kept in the ice box. It is a few years before pasteurized milk is delivered in glass bottles and is kept in an electric refrigerator.*]

By 10 o'clock we are all downtown to watch the parade. Fourth of July is the day to celebrate patriotism, which we all do with great fervor. It is only ten years since America fought The-War-To- End-All-Wars, and now our flag is a symbol for Peace in the world!

We are a town of 10,000 people, and this is the county seat, with an imposing courthouse on its own city block in the middle of town. Families piled into farmers' wagons are thronging the streets and getting settled down to watch the parade. There is a flag in front of every store, and little handheld flags waving everywhere. My dad owns the shoe store right across the street from the courthouse, and we are sitting on the curb as the parade approaches.

The band plays, loudly and proudly, a favorite John Philip Sousa march. The drum major leads, strutting and prancing, as the marching musicians toot and whistle and beat their way along the street, with everyone cheering and waving. I am filled with pride at being part of this town. Then come marching army veterans in uniform, two pushed in wheelchairs.

I feel the powerful wave of emotion as bugles sound, and the big billowing American flag approaches, the biggest I have ever seen. It is carried by a strong handsome smartly uniformed young soldier. The cheer that bursts from my throat joins the hundreds of others all along the street as I am completely one with all the people of my town. "Hooray, hooray, hooray." Men toss their straw hats in the air, and we stamp our feet and cheer and cheer and cheer. It is a glorious feeling. I get moist eyes as I remember the poem I had learned at school:

Hats off! Along the street there comes
The blare of bugles, the ruffle of drums,
A flash of color beneath the sky.
Hats off! The flag is passing by!

At school we begin every day with the salute to the flag. Every classroom has one. We stand beside our desks facing the flag, right hand over the heart, and earnestly say together:

" I pledge allegiance to my flag and to the republic for which it stands.

One nation, indivisible, with liberty and justice for all."

[In later years the Congress tampered with the words of the Pledge, but our words were the "real ones." It's amazing to me now that I am 93 years old, how much emotion that memory holds for me, of pride in my identity with my flag. Of course this was the 48-star flag, and I still think it was the prettiest one. Well, the feeling of patriotism in those days was fine and strong, and I am glad it was part of my life.]

The parade ends with the band, still playing, filing into the bandstand on the corner of the courthouse grounds.

[Every town had a city band, and a bandstand, either by the courthouse or in a city park. This was when recorded music and the wind-up Victrola were new and scarce, and the infant radio didn't yet play any music, so

LIVE music was still a vital part of human life. The Bandmaster was an important city employee. The musicians were paid by the city to play for every occasion.]

Today the bandstand is draped with red-white-and-blue bunting. The band plays several pieces, and a soprano sings with a full voice. Then a politician makes a stirring speech about the League of Nations, and a future of world peace. Of course the only way of increasing the volume of his voice is with a handheld megaphone (no electronics yet exist), but people applaud, even if they can't hear what he says.

The crowd begins to break up and mill around, friends and relatives embracing and kissing, men shaking hands and patting backs, children snatching things from one another and running away laughing. It is a happy crowd. The mid-1920s are good times. Farmers are thriving, merchants are prospering, women are finding new freedoms, there are exciting new inventions. The town is growing, as new houses are being built. Anything could happen.

Back home we pick juicy ripe apricots from the tree in the back yard, and there are peanut butter sandwiches and milk. Then sweaty drowsy children lie down on the cool hardwood floor, to nap beside the oscillating electric fan. The temperature is in the high 90s.

When we wake, Mother and Daddy are loading picnic things into the big red Buick touring car. We drive a few miles beyond the edge of town to Lindsay bridge, where we join the Whiddons and the Bentleys and the Woodruffs and all their kids. This has long been a favorite picnic place, where Pecan Creek is wide and shallow, with sandy flat edges. The high rocky banks are edged with big shade

68

trees: pecan, hickory, and hackberry trees, with sassafras and little wild plum trees mixed in. Squirrels scurry and leap through the limbs, chittering and flicking their fluffy tails, while birds chirp and flutter around. Wild grape vines cover the embankment, sheltering lizards and hornytoads. Right at the bridge the creek is narrower, and four or five feet deep, making a good swimming-hole. The adults spread out old army blankets on the sandy shore, set up folding card tables to serve the food, and the men start turning the cranks of the ice cream freezers. All the kids are in the creek.

"Watch out for the poison oak," calls out one mother. We well know that here there are cottonmouth water moccasins (poisonous snakes). We kids spend much of our time exploring the woods and creeks at the edges of our neighborhoods, so we recognize these dangers by the time we are three years old. I am already six in 1927, and I can take care of myself! Anyway, I have Townsend, who has always been my stalwart and reliable protector and guide. Little boys are drilled in being "manly," which includes being responsible for "women-folks," and behaving courteously. So there is much splashing and shoving in the shallow water; but when it becomes too rowdy, all that is needed is for one of the dads to walk over with an upraised hand, and the roughness abates. It's still joyful and fun.

[*It is interesting to remember what bathing suits were like. All of them were made of thick wool from the shoulders to a couple of inches below the crotch. Both male and female. It was years before men wore swim "trunks" with white knit cotton tank tops. I was adult before the top was abandoned and men went bare from the waist up; and that was considered scandalous for a time. Even after that,*

69

women's suits were still one-piece with a little skirt for modesty.]

The picnic is wonderful. All the families share all the food. Picnic plates have already been invented, plain white paper with crimped edges. But we use metal forks, knives and spoons, and tin cups. Big thermos jugs, with pouring spouts, hold lemonade and iced tea. The ice-man delivers ice to our kitchen, and we use ice picks to chip it small, to get it into the big jug.

[I never saw anyone drinking wine or beer or any alcohol until after Prohibition was over. There truly were millions of people in America who were contented to avoid alcohol.]

The tables are loaded with big platters of fried chicken, potato salad, coleslaw, sliced fresh tomatoes, cucumber slices soaked in vinegar, deviled eggs, homemade biscuits. Of course there are big watermelons to cut into. When we have all gorged ourselves with this delicious food, there are the angel food and devil's food cakes with thick frosting, not to forget the absolutely fabulous hand-cranked ice cream, made with homegrown peaches and pecans! (How my mouth waters when I remember.) No one has ever heard of diets. We just really enjoy our fabulous food.

A rest time follows, stretched out on the blankets, lulled by mockingbirds, the buzz of locusts and the gurgling creek. We drowse in the heat, happy in the closeness of dear ones.

As afternoon shadows lengthen, we gather everything up and go back to town.

With the day darkening, there are the real fireworks. There are magnificently colored rockets arching through the sky. There is a tower of pinwheels, of rainbow colors, each pinwheel, as it finishes burning, setting off the next one, circling up the tower.

I fall asleep on the back seat of the Buick, not even aware, later, of being carried in to my bed. It had been a long memorable Fourth of July, that we had begun by being the FIRST ONES to set off firecrackers. In my dream I hear pop pop pop pop pop …

~ 14 ~
THOSE OTHERS

My daughter, Louise, had a group of loyal friends, from age 13 on through high school. One of these friends was Beverly. I never knew her family well, but I knew she was born to older parents. Her mother, Peggy, was a stay-at-home mom. The older sister was married and lived nearby. The retired father had been a successful business man, and they were a conservative family living in a large house in a good neighborhood near Land Park in Sacramento. We and the other parents did not socialize together, but we felt it was good to keep in touch and agree about rules and activities for our kids. They were not difficult kids. They were busy about interesting activities. Then when they were 15, a tragedy struck. Beverley's dad was marching in the St. Patrick's Day parade, and he fell dead on the street.

It was the first time for any of the girls to experience tragedy, and all the changes it brought in every level of daily life. I had a busy job in the state capitol, but I formed a habit of just phoning Peggy every now and then. She would talk about having to learn for the first time about the family finances and business arrangements. Being responsible for decisions, about the home property, and about Beverly, all seemed overwhelming to Peggy.

After about six months, Peggy told me she was deciding to sell the house. She and Bev would move into a smaller place that they would rent. It would all be easier for her. It was 1963, an era when finding a new place to live would not be hard. So Bev and her mother were apartment hunting. Bev was feeling the distress of deciding which childhood treasures she could bear to discard, to move into a smaller space.

Peggy told me on the phone, "The realtor won't let me be in the house when anyone comes to look at it! It already feels like it isn't even my house anymore."

"Yes I've heard of that. You wonder what they are saying about your house that they don't want you to hear." She said, "You wonder what they think you might say that they don't want the buyers to know."

One day Beverly came over and told us it was sold. "But wait 'til you see the great place we're moving to! And I get to pick the new furniture for my room. Mom says I get to choose everything for my room." The girls went off to squeal and scream and giggle over catalogues and advertisements. I called Peggy to hear the good news.

"Yeah it's all signed and sealed. The realtor got what we were asking, and everything checks out. They're moving here from Los Angeles, a young couple with a little boy and a baby on the way. He has a new job here. Next week they're coming to the house to look at the furniture and things I'm selling, to see what they might want to keep in the house. I haven't met them yet. They'll take possession in three months." She went on to tell me about the new place they'd be moving into. I was happy for her. There had been many times when she had sounded lonely and overwhelmed.

The next week Bev told us, "The people who're buying our house are coming tomorrow, but I'll be at school. I won't even see them. It feels weird that they'll be standing in my room, and figuring out how they're going to change everything, so that a little boy can live there!"

Louise put her arm around her friend. "Does that not feel good to you?" Bev leaned on her shoulder.

"Yeah. It's been my room all my life. It's my place! . I don't want it to be for someone else. And a little boy. Ugh! It'll be a mess. He'll probably have toads in there."

"Aw, well, he might," I laughed.

Louise gave her a squeeze. "You're going to have your beautiful new room. You'll have so much fun fixing it up."

I added, "You've outgrown your childhood room now. It's a fine time of your life to make a new place for yourself."

Next day when I got home from work Peggy called me. "Oh Beth, it's awful!"

"What? Are they backing out of the sale?"

"Oh, no," she said. "Oh, I wish they would! No, they're all excited. No, Beth!" She began to cry. "They're black," sobbing.

"What?" Silence except for sobs. "They are colored people. There are going to be colored people living in my house!"

"Oh. I see … well, that is a surprise."

I did not share her feelings. I was an active Democrat, Unitarian, descended from many generations of Quakers. I would have welcomed black neighbors myself, but actually there were none in our neighborhood. The junior high school down the street had not one black child.

That was 1963. Although I bit my tongue and did not tell her so, the truth is I felt scornful of her attitude, and after that I talked with Peggy only about our daughters.

Well, dear reader, there is another episode in this story. I got my come-uppance.

The girls went on and graduated from high school. Louise went off to college at Reed. My house was still busy with people involved in various activities to save the world. Then Ronny Reagan ran for Governor of California, and to my horror he was elected! Republicans began to move into the Capitol building and turn our good government programs upside down!

I had an opportunity to go to work in Washington D.C., so I decided to go. With Louise away at college, I had been living alone with my cat in the three-bedroom rented house. I had loved our house. I was devoted to my garden. But I had reached the point in my career to move up professionally. Louise came home for the summer, and we sorted through the lifetime accumulation of things, discarding and packing up. A very emotional time, of course, with new plans for each of us, going very separate ways for the first time in her life.

The owner of the house was ready to advertise it for rent, and he asked me if I minded if he brought people to see it. "No, just let me know when. And you realize everything will be a mess."

Several people came. Then it was decided: this couple, with a child, would be the ones. They came back later, to measure spaces, and we chatted. That is when I learned: he was coming to work in the Governor's office. They were of the "radical right!"

When they left the house, I sat and thought of Those People, whose energy was going to fill the spaces where my good Liberal friends had held so many potluck dinners and animated discussions, and hatched so many good ideas for more effective government. I was horrified.

After while, the memory came to me of when Peggy had discovered that "black people" had bought her house. She couldn't bear the thought that her spaces would be occupied by Those Others. Now how did I feel?

We find all kinds of reasons in life to make ourselves separate from Those Others, one way or another.

NATURAL CHILDBIRTH IN 1948

"Oh, whatever name you want, dear, I'll be happy with whatever you want," Ted assures me, holding me close beside him .

"No! Whatever you want. If it's a boy, you should name him," with my cheek on his shoulder.

Of course we are driving to the hospital, and, although we've decided on Carol Louise, we have never quite settled on a name for a boy. (In 1948 it wasn't possible to learn ahead of time what the gender was.) Neither of us has much experience with hospitals, but we feel confident of Dr. Preece, and Mercer County Hospital (Trenton, N.J.) has a good reputation.

Three months into my pregnancy someone had given me a book to read. Written by an English obstetrician, it was called Childbirth Without Fear. It is hard to imagine now, but in 1948 there was not a single American book about natural childbirth. I read the book eagerly, and tried to discuss it with other young women, but didn't find much interest. The common practice was to go to a hospital where you were given ether, which put you to sleep, to escape the pain of giving birth. That is how I was born, as were all the children I grew up with.

From the time I learned where babies came from (not the stork) this had always seemed wrong to me. I had been taken to the hospital to see a newborn cousin. The mother was asleep when the baby was born. When she woke, they told her whether it was a boy or a girl, whether it had dark hair or blonde or was bald, what weight it was. Everyone else already knew all about it: the doctor and the nurses, the daddy and the grandmother, the baby's older siblings, even other patients in the hospital. Everyone knew all about it while the mother was still asleep.

As a little girl I thought this was all wrong. When I had a baby, I wanted to be there when this big wonderful event happened. I didn't want to miss out on it, and have other people just tell me about it. Of course it was explained to me that the reason was because it was such horrible pain that the mother would have. It was the worst pain imaginable, and it just went on and on, until finally the baby was born. Then you'd be so exhausted that you didn't want to do anything but rest. With ether, you could just sleep through it, and then enjoy your baby when you woke.

It made sense. Everybody made a very big thing about what an awful experience was this terrible pain of childbirth. It always seemed a bit exaggerated to me. I thought it would be worse to miss the glorious excitement of the new baby appearing.

Perhaps it was partly because I had never experienced any really significant pain in my life. I was an adventurous child. Satisfying my curiosity was of much much greater importance to me than a skinned knee or a bruised elbow. When I came to menstruation I'd had only the mildest of cramps. I had watched the pregnant cat seeking a cozy corner. Then I had knelt beside her, entranced, as she squeezed out one kitten after another. She had seemed anxious while seeking her nest, but not during the actual birthing. And once the kittens started suckling, she'd settled back and purred and purred, licking them lovingly.

Then I had seen puppies born, and even saw a calf struggle out into the world. Clearly the mother animals were experiencing an ordeal, but not this "horrible" drama that a woman would be desperate to escape from. And I saw the obvious happiness in bonding with the newborn!

It all puzzled me.

In the mid 1940s the "new" method of childbirth that was eagerly sought was called "saddle block," which, as I understood it, numbed all sensation in the pelvic area while the baby was being born. My sister-in-law had just had her baby this way shortly before I became pregnant; so I had heard about it, and thought I might do that. But I still felt doubtful about the need to "escape" the natural experience.

So this book rang true for me. The general theme was that "fear makes pain, and then pain makes fear." Dr. Grantly Dick Reed described how, in England in the early 20th century, many women still had babies at home, often with a midwife. More and more, any woman who could afford it went to a doctor in a hospital, and was given ether. Even if the doctor went to a home birth, he usually gave ether. But when the mother was thus sedated, the baby also was sedated. Often that baby had a slow start. It had become normal practice to slap the baby into taking its first breath. Dr. Reed had found that when the mother's attitude was less fearful, she had less pain. The more she regarded birthing as a natural process, which included calling it "sensation" rather than "pain," the more she could relax into just working at it.

The word "labor" is really correct. It is hard work, and it is using muscles that are not otherwise exercised. You can't just "decide" to stop and rest. The labor process goes on, and keeps on, and on and on and on and on, until its mission is complete.

All of this sounded really correct to me. Ted, always interested in new ideas, and pleased that I was exploring the possibilities of my new experience, was also eager for his child to have the best possible start in life.

When I went back to Dr. Preece for my regular appointment, I took the book with me. I pushed it across his desk and asked, "Do you know about this book?" He said "Yes."

I said, "Well I'm interested. How do you feel about it?" He said, "I'm interested."

I knew that the hospital was a teaching hospital and that he was a professor of obstetrics. I asked, "Have you tried this approach?" "No, I haven't."

I could see I had his full attention. "Well, I'd like to try it. What do you think?" He said, "I'd really like to try."

He made sure that I understood that neither he nor anyone in the hospital had had any experience with these ideas, and we would be experimenting; but they would be ready with their usual routine if I changed my mind. I was more and more sure.

In the wee hours of the morning of Sept. 30,1948, I was wakened by strange sensations in my abdomen. I shook my husband awake. We hugged each other with excitement, and busied ourselves with calling the doctor and leaving the house. It was just three days earlier than the predicted date.

We were at the hospital an hour before Dr. Preece arrived, and the head nurse was impatient to start the routine injections, etc. They had banished Ted to the waiting room, put me to bed in one of those open-back short white garments, given me an enema, and had shaved the pubic hair. Dr. Preece tried to explain to the staff how we were not going to be doing the usual routine. He got only doubtful looks, and I heard mutterings of, "Just wait. She'll ask for it."

The labor stopped, and started again, several times. They put me in a wheelchair and took me out to visit my anxious husband. There my water broke, and they took me back to my room, where labor began in earnest. It was indeed hard work and very tiring, and you can't do anything to stop and rest or make it easier, except to relax muscles that are not involved. It was some years later that they came up with breathing practices. In the 1940s no member of the family was allowed anywhere near.

By this time on that day, the nurses' attitude is becoming at least interested. After 11 hours, finally I am taken into the delivery room. I have to admit that the process of dilation is "uncomfortable." When the baby's head is actually scraping through the pelvic bones … well, it is painful. But brief.

The delivery room is crowded, all the staff coming to see this crazy lady who wants to give birth without anesthetic. There are two resident doctors, several interns, all the nurses and student nurses, even the charwoman. (But the husband is not allowed.)

There's a mirror positioned so the anesthetist stationed beside me (just in case) could see the baby's head appear. So I can watch too. My wrists are tied down at my sides (their standard procedure, because all the other women had been sedated). Dr. Preece is lecturing, as usual, and I can hear, of course. I am very distracted, but he is talking about what I am doing.

Finally the head is out ….

Then the final great push—the most vastly ecstatic exultant orgasm imaginable.

And Dr. Preece is holding up the baby to show me. He says, "Here is your little girl, Mrs. Gawain." MY LITTLE GIRL. She is vocalizing lustily, exploring the new experience of making sound with her own voice.

Dr. Preece says to the assembled crowd, "You see this baby was not sedated, because the mother was not sedated. This baby needs no help to start to breathe." They applaud.

So here she is, my precious little baby girl, living and breathing. And I am indeed right here to receive her. I am so happy to be fully present and aware, in this incomparable moment.

~ 16 ~
BIRTHDAY IN SRI LANKA

"It's your birthday. What do you want to do?" Ann asked me, over breakfast tea with toast and mango jam. I said, "Mmm, let's consider the possibilities."

"Count me in," said Blake. "I'd be happy to help with whatever you decide."

"Actually, I'm tired from travelling," I admitted. "I'd like to mostly just explore around here today: the lakefront and the little shrines and old shops."

Just the night before we had arrived in Kandy, the ancient capital of the island kingdom of Sri Lanka, off the southern tip of India. We were almost on the equator, but up here at the higher altitude of Kandy, although it was languidly warm, it was not the oppressive steamy heat of the coastal areas.

"I know what I'd like to do in the late afternoon is to go down to the river when they bring the working elephants to bathe in the water." We had heard about that from other travelers. "Oh, yes, yes," they both agreed.

I was turning 54 years old. I was into the second month of a proposed whole year of travel and study around India, Sri Lanka and Nepal. I had made only outline plans, going day to day spontaneously. On my third day of arrival in Bombay, I had met Ann, staying in the Red Shield Hostel. She was a 32-year-old biology teacher at a San Francisco Bay Area college. Blake was a 28-year-old Canadian teaching high school drama. We were all heading south from Bombay and decided to travel together. It was working out very well indeed. Years later I would receive a letter from Blake saying, "What an unlikely trio we were, and what fun we had!"

For that first day in Kandy we by-passed visiting the famous Temple of the Tooth, so-named because it houses an actual tooth of the real Buddha. (Really?) The next day we planned to watch the annual parade of temple elephants, gorgeously caparisoned with ornately decorated robes of rich fabrics. One elephant would carry grandly on its back the bejeweled little chest containing the tooth itself. The parade would also include the famous Kandy Dancers, marvelously acrobatic men and women in fabulous costumes, who would follow the elephants through the streets, performing their traditional extraordinary dance as they went.

Now that I am 92 years old, I don't remember all of that birthday long ago. I do remember the streets were busy with colorfully clad, easy-going people , including many pleasant-voiced children. The lake was large and calm, bordered, waist-high, by an ancient serrated white stone wall. Big old trees, shading wooden benches, formed a lakeside park.

In that mid-day Ann and I had enjoyed browsing in a bookshop on the lakefront. I still have the little book she bought me for a present. It explains Theravada Buddhism as it is practiced in Sri Lanka, and in India and Burma. It's the form of Buddhism I have always found most comfortable for me.

We were to meet Blake outside in the park. He saw us and beckoned us over to join him in the pleasant shade at one of the benches. We settled down gratefully. "Are you ready for your birthday?" he asked me.

"Oh. Well, yes, I guess I'm ready." Blake reached around behind the bench and pulled out a birthday cake … with lighted candles! Imagine! (I never did figure out how he managed those lighted candles. It must have been a completely windless day.) They sang, "Happy birthday to you," and it truly was a very happy day.

We did go down to the river when they brought the elephants, to bathe at the end of the day's work. The scene was quite joyous. The elephants (I think 7 of them) were trotting eagerly as they approached the water, and the men rode them, splashing hugely, into the river. As the men leaped off, the beasts rolled over to immerse themselves, emitting happy groans. They filled their trunks with water, and sprayed themselves. And sprayed each other. They sprayed the men, who splashed them back. They sprayed the laughing children gathered at the bank.

"Oops!" Blake had snatched me back a few steps, but not quite quickly enough! A spray from one of the elephants had been expertly aimed at us, and had succeeded in reaching our bare legs. The delighted twinkle in the elephant's eye made it well worth a drenching.

My inner spirit really did jump into the fray, where wet mounds of tumbling bodies were festooned with sparkling diamond droplets, accompanied by contented beastly rumbles, and joyful human shouts and laughter.

As the energy waned, and the great beasts were slowly rolling in the water, the men began to scrub the tough skin with big heavy brushes. The huge grey bodies lolled back in the shallows with deep mellow moans, the small eyes taking on an expression of utter bliss.

A most carefree, playful, happy scene. That is how I remember my 54th birthday, in Sri Lanka.

~ 17 ~
FIRE WALK

It has to be a trick. Some sort of slight-of-hand. (Or slight-of-foot?) There's no way that a bare foot could walk on hot coals and not be burned. But my friend, Deva, was seriously proposing that we do it.

"You know Tony," she reminded me. "He and his wife and some others are living way up in the woods now. They've studied how, for eons, fire walking has been done in Asia and the Pacific islands. A couple of years ago Tony started doing it himself, and then showing other people. I went and watched. Then last year I went again, and I did it!"

Wow! She had walked on fire herself.

I was staying with Deva for a month in her cabin in the old California gold country. She had received notice that these old friends were scheduling another fire walk this Saturday, and she had said to me, "Let's go." I had long heard of fire walking, but never even imagined myself doing it. And to have to decide right now? I was very hesitant.

"What's this, Beth? I think of you as being one of the most adventurous people I know. Ready for anything."

"Oh come on, Deva. You know I won't even do alcohol or tobacco, or anything that I regard as harmful. How could anybody really walk barefoot on red-hot coals? Don't you just imagine that you've done it, after some hypnosis or something?"

So she sat me down and told me in detail about her own personal experience of walking on the red-hot coals.

She named other friends of ours who had done it, and would be there tomorrow.

"But how does it work?"

"Beth, I don't know. The rational mind just can't accept it. That's why it's such an adventure. You can come and watch tomorrow. Even that is an education, because it is unbelievable. I guess I'm glad that at my age I can confront my rational mind with something unbelievable."

We were 60 years old. Most of these other friends were more than 25-years-younger than we were. But no one was going to think of us as old fogeys. So we went.

We drove on up into the mountains on country lanes. Our old friend Tony had several acres of woods and meadows around the comfortable old house he had bought. On this day, there were maybe 30 people, some to help set everything up, some to take the walk, some who just wanted to watch. The big fire was already started, to create the hot coals. The straight bare-earth walkway was maybe 25 feet long and two feet wide, dug down to an even depth, to hold the hot coals, which would be evenly spread.

The ten of us who were doing the walk were required to come to an introduction, inside the house with Tony. Deva was there, and two other people I knew. We were shown some home movies of people doing the fire walk. There were close-up views of the glowing coals, and of the faces of people about to set foot on them. Then there were scenes of people walking on the hot coals, both close-up and of the big scene, from beginning to end of the walk. There were interviews of people who had completed the walk, expressing their amazement and incredulity at what they had just done, and showing their feet unharmed. After the film, two people who had done the walk before talked about their experience. We were invited to ask questions. No one offered any explanation of how it happened. They simply attested that it did happen to them.

Tony himself repeatedly said, "I have no explanation, only that it does work."

But not quite always.

We were shown instances when someone had been hurt. Invariably, it was when they had doubts about their own safety, but had walked anyway. So the crucially important rule was:

WHEN YOU ARE FIRST ABOUT TO SET FOOT ON THE COALS, TAKE STOCK OF YOURSELF. "AM I READY?" IF YOU FEEL DOUBT, DON'T WALK.

"Just step aside and let the next person go," Tony told us.

"You can try again later, when you've watched other people more. Or maybe never. But it's crucial to follow, at that moment, your own intuition."

We had been told to bring our own bottle or thermos of water to drink. They did not give us anything to eat or drink, so there was no possibility that they had "doped" us . There was no mention of spiritual beings or sacred practices, no mystique. Nor was there any emotional workup, with chanting or drumming or dancing. All was just perfectly simple and matter-of-fact. And rational!

So what shall I do?

Clearly many people had walked on fiery coals without harm.

I thought, "It must be that the mind has so much control over the body that ... *what we expect the body to do* ... that is what will really happen. It's this hour spent convincing the rational mind ... that's what makes it happen. What I <u>expect</u> to experience, that's what I will experience.

"What do I now expect? *I expect that my feet will be uncomfortably hot, but I will not be harmed.*

"So I will walk."

When we went back outside, darkness had fallen. The fire-tenders were very quickly raking the glowing hot coals into the long shallow pit that formed the walkway. People who had come to watch were sitting silently about ten feet back along the way. Several were people I knew.

We took off our shoes and socks and left them on a bench. We clustered near the Start, while the red coals were smoothly raked into place. We could feel the heat on our bare faces and arms. No question but these were very hot coals. We were given our last instructions.

1. Remember, the most important thing of all is: just before you step on to the path, check with your inner self: "Am I ready to do this?" If your body starts forward, then just go! If there is any hesitation, step aside and walk away. You can try again later if you want to, or not.

2. Once you do start, look forward and step straight along steadily, not hurrying but moving smoothly right along to the end, and continue off onto the ground.

3. You are free to step off to the side onto the ground at any time, just quit and walk away. If you feel moved to do that, don't hesitate to quit. No problem.

"Who wants to go first?" The whole place was perfectly silent. I felt that all of us were very deeply tuned within.

One of the men who had done it before took his place at the Start, paused for a deep breath, then stepped out onto the glowing coals, and walked and walked and steadily went on. There were gasps at the first step, then absolute silence until he stepped off onto the ground at the end, and a few more paces. He looked down at his feet. Clearly they were not hurt.

There were murmurs all around. But already the next person had started, and was walking purposefully forward along the radiant path, to the end. Then it was Deva. Then my other friend, George. It was happening. It was happening just like the film.

As the seventh person, I find myself at the Start. "Am I ready?" I ask deep within. There is no hesitation at all. My body moves forward, and my bare feet are walking, one foot after the other, moving along perfectly naturally, on this glowing path. I am walking on fire!

I feel the firm lumpiness of the coals I'm walking on, but I am astonished to feel <u>no heat</u>! I had believed that it would feel hot.

I continue placing one step after step after step onward on the coals. Just before I reach the end, there is a sudden hot spot on my left instep, up higher toward my ankle than where my soles are touching the lumps!

Now I have reached the end, and have stepped onto the bare earth. Someone has taken hold of me and is leading me to a bench. I have done it ...

I look at the soles of my feet. They are perfectly normal pale skin, not burned at all.

I have walked on the hot coals and am not harmed. There is this one, quarter-inch spot, just above my left instep, where some spark must have flown up from the hotbed, and burned my skin. Yet the feet that had been set down firmly and repeatedly on that hot bed did <u>not</u> get burned ... How is that contradiction possible? More mystery.

What I had (ahead of time) believed to be the explanation was this: "My body will do what the mind expects."

I had expected that my feet would be numb, and somehow the numbness would prevent burning. But they were not numb. I did feel the lumpiness of the coals as I put my full weight on each foot repeatedly. What I had expected is not what happened.

"It boggles my mind." That is a super under-statement. My rational mind is ... well ... "It's in tatters" would be a description.

"Was your life affected by this experience?" a friend asked me. Yes, I think so.

"If you have an experience that doesn't make sense to the rational mind, 'it isn't reality.' It didn't really happen. But it DID happen to me. The impossible did happen.

"Are we so fixed on the reality of rationality that we are missing out on some possible life experiences? Yes, after this experience, I do think so."

~ 18 ~
DEMONSTRATING

By the time Louise was 10 years old I had been taking her with me to demonstrations for peace and justice. All her life she had heard these issues discussed, both in our family and among our friends. At the time when some of our neighbors were digging backyard bomb shelters (fearing an atomic bomb explosion) she had created a poster for art class saying, "THE ONLY SHELTER IS PEACE."

When she was in high school in Sacramento we would make our cardboard signs for nonviolence, attach them to sticks, and go to picket on the steps of the state capitol. She had learned that, as long as you kept moving, you couldn't be arrested.

The other night we were recalling that. She said, "Remember the time when, I guess there was a sit-in for some cause, inside the State capitol rotunda. We were shifting around in the close-packed crowd, and I found myself ... right next to ... Paul Newman and Marlon Brando!! Wow."

"Oh yes!" I remembered. " Both so, so handsome! Both had make-up on, because there were news cameras."

"I remember that I was a little disappointed to see how short they were!" she said.

"Oh, yeah, they were not tall men. And you had already grown to your full height. I'm reminded of when I grew to 5'8" when I was only 11 years old! It was shocking to find that many adults were not very big."

In late September, 1966, Louise went off to Reed College in Portland Oregon, just a week before she would turn 18 years old. Back in Sacramento, a few days after her departure, I was relaxing from my day's work, with the cat in my lap, watching the Huntley Brinkley news, when there was a story about the police in Portland, Oregon. It showed the paddy-wagon with helmeted policemen piling out, nightsticks in hand, to go quell a demonstration outside a hotel where a political campaign speech was scheduled.

An hour later, I was eating my dinner when the telephone rang. "Yes, I am Mrs. Gawain." Then the woman said, "I'm calling from the police station in Portland, Oregon. We have here your daughter, Louise."

"Oh my! Has she been in an accident? Is she hurt?" The woman answered, "Oh, she's not hurt . We're not sure if the policeman she struck may be hurt!"

"What? She hit a policeman?" It took a bit of effort to get the details of what happened, which I then put together with what I had seen on the news. Louise had been among the demonstrators when the police were swinging their billy-clubs against her new Reed friends, and she had lowered her sign down on a policeman's head. I said on the phone, "You're telling me that a skinny 17-year-old girl hit the man's helmeted head with her cardboard sign, and you don't know if he's hurt?" (I don't suppose my attitude was any help to her situation.)

Now that she is 65 and I am 92, we are remembering this drama. She tells me, "The policeman I hit didn't even notice me. He was focused on kicking my friend, who was sitting on the ground. Kicking hard in the abdomen with his heavy boot! I was yelling, 'Stop that. stop that!' The sign I was holding up over us … well it was just so easy to lower it down on his head. It was another policeman who saw me do it. He came over and grabbed me, and hustled me to the police wagon. I was crying and saying, 'I didn't mean to do it!' He said, 'Yes you did, you little phony.' He shoved me into the wagon with several others.

"Oh, Mom, I was so scared. I couldn't believe I had hit a policeman, and with my nonviolence sign! I never would have imagined that anyone could do anything to provoke me to do such a thing."

We both pondered that for a moment. I said, "That was a really shocking provocation; you could never have imagined a policeman doing that, kicking your friends."

She went on, "Then at the police station, they found that I was a minor—for three more days, until my 18th birthday. They couldn't charge me. But they separated me from all the others. That was the worst thing. They put me in a room by myself, and just left me there alone for a long, long time."

How awful, we agreed.

Finally, the Dean at Reed College had learned what was happening, and had come to take care of the situation. He phoned me. I was so relieved to hear that he had taken her safely back to her dorm room, where her suitemates clustered anxiously around.

Because she was a minor, there could be no record of her transgression. What good fortune that she had those three more days before turning 18. Striking a policeman is a truly serious offense.

Louise never again carried a protest sign. No, never again.

~ 19 ~
A WEALTH OF TIME

One of the many rewarding aspects of growing older is that we begin to "have time." For so many many years, there were so many many occasions when the conversation had centered around some new interest that we would have loved to follow, but ... there would be a big sigh, and then, "I just don't have time."

There were those moments when your spouse, or your child, or your co-worker, or your secretary would say, "You said you were going to do that yesterday!"

"Yes, I know. I just didn't have time."

It is a marvelous luxury, after we retire, to wake in the morning and be able to decide, on the spur of the moment, "What do I want to do this morning?" And, maybe, even again in the same afternoon. "What would I like to do now?" Imagine. No schedule.

When I stopped working in my career as a city planner, one of the first things I did was to get a bird book. Then I persuaded my niece, Leah (who was educated as a naturalist), to take me bird watching. I had always been interested in birds, but she had to show me the simplest things. Such as how to see the birds among the leaves or grasses. (You watch for movement in the foliage, then focus there.) At first I used my heirloom mother-of-pearl opera glasses to go bird watching. Then, after two years of travelling the globe, as I was shopping for the next trip, I saw a small pair of binoculars really meant for outdoor watching. They were as small (for packing) as the opera glasses. Now, after many years of using them, I have a long list of birds on five continents that I've had the joy of watching.

Another thing I'd wanted to learn was watercolor painting. So a few years later I did that. I took up yoga practice. I joined a choral group and sang tenor in 4-part harmony.

After I was 70, I learned to throw pottery, and made bowls and vases, and even a bird-bath for my garden in Hawai'i. I learned sculpture with clay, and still keep some of the clay faces I created. In my mid-80s, I joined Community Theatre, took a character part in a play, and loved when everyone laughed and applauded.

I did it all at leisurely pace, when the spirit moved me.

It was a glorious feeling to have time to do all these things without crowding them into an already over-busy schedule. I remember, a few years into my retirement (maybe 1980), my daughter Shakti (no longer called Louise) became a devotee of the Day-Timer. It was a then-popular pocket-size booklet for keeping track of all your appointments. She gave me one for Christmas, and enthusiastically began showing me how to use it. I was overwhelmed with RESISTANCE. The last thing in the world I wanted to do was to fill my life with schedules. It was hard for her to grasp that. I had always been this mother with a busy career, and multiple other interests.

I remember once when she was in second grade, and at dinnertime the sitter arrived. My little girl looked at me appealingly and said, "Are you going to another meeting tonight?" I'm afraid that, in addition to the night meetings, I customarily wrote speeches on weekends, and did the newsletter for Parents Without Partners, and was vice president of the Co-op. Now, when I meet people who knew me in those years, they will say, "What are you doing these days?" My favorite answer is, "As little as possible." Another good answer is in Italian: "Dolce far niente." (Sweet to do nothing.)

That brings us to the most important point of this discourse: Having time to do things that I'd never "had time for" is a great freedom. But the greatest freedom of all is the freedom to <u>choose</u> occasionally to do … nothing.

Now, doing nothing, especially in our busy culture, is not easy. It requires a big shift in <u>values</u>, and a significant change of <u>habits</u>. And then … it requires practice. The impulse to start DOING SOMETHING … ANYTHING … is very powerful at first.

A great way to begin, I think, is with nature. I could easily spend half an hour just sitting in my outdoor chair and watching the trees swaying in the breeze. Or watching ants. A favorite thing would be to watch raindrops on big banana leaves, each water-drop beading like quicksilver. Of course most visitors to a seashore have discovered the magic of watching ocean waves wash in and out, in and out, each time just a l i t t l e bit different. My whole soul gets into the primordial rhythm of it. I like to feel that I can do nothing, not even meditate.

I believe it is important for us who are elders to be an example in the world of taking great pleasure in quiet time. Our culture has so little silence, so much noise and busy-ness. The standard greeting is "How're ya <u>doing</u>?" or "What've you been up to?" Even the classic greeting when being formally introduced was "How do you <u>do</u>?" When someone has actually been sick we may ask, "How are you <u>feeling</u>?" (And then we hope they won't go on and on about it.)

At least now we often say, "How are you?" But the expected answer is really just,

"I'm fine." (Do you ever feel that they actually want to hear how you are?)

Does anyone ever ask, "What have you been wondering about?" Or "What fantasies have you been dreaming up?"

Our culture places so much value on eventfulness and excitement! Can we value silence, peace, serenity? Can we take time for that?

As we grow really older, we get slower. Routine things, that we've always done, take more time to do. Just getting up, making the bed, getting washed and dressed and down to breakfast … well, it takes much longer. Being slower, about everything, does melt away some of that wealth of time. Impatience and frustration with our own new clumsiness and pokiness take a toll on our peace of mind. It's OK to remember, wistfully, how quick we used to be! Now we need to expect less of ourselves.

Can we have a life that has balance among: (1) doing the things that require our attention, and (2) engaging in planned activities, and (3) leaving unplanned time? Time for choosing, spontaneously, to do something we enjoy … or … choosing to just be easy?

To just BE …?

Elder years can bring a wealth of time for going places and doing things we couldn't do in years of career and family responsibilities. On the other hand, it also allows us to take quiet time. Now we have a wealth of time for contemplation, and silence.

We have time to drift in being.

~ 20 ~
ALL I WANT IS RINGO

When my niece, Elaine, was fourteen, she came to live with my sixteen year old daughter and me, for one school year in Sacramento. Louise and I were living in a pleasant 3-bedroom house on the tree-lined older part of Land Park Drive.

It was 1964, the time of Beatlemania. Louise seemed most drawn to John, I found Paul interesting, while Elaine was an avid fan of Ringo. She used a radio station to keep track of where in the world he was every single day. Of course both girls played the records repeatedly. I enjoyed the songs, and often joined them in singing along.

As December approached I asked the girls what they would particularly like for Christmas. Louise had wishes that were within my capability, and I began to work on my plans for her. Elaine was different. With clasped hands and a soulful deep sigh she would say, "All I want is Ringo!" That was the only answer I could get, from several tries.

How can I give her Ringo? Of course she has all the records, and the walls of her room are plastered with pictures of Ringo.

I conceived the idea of making her a Ringo rag-doll, and decided to explore that possibility. I wondered if I might even make it life size. Wouldn't that be something? I was skilled at sewing, and enjoyed a challenge. I found a pattern for a Raggedy Andy doll, and set about making the pattern pieces much larger.

It was surprisingly easy to find out exactly how tall Ringo was, and I went on from there. I bought a Beatle wig from the local costume shop. I found flesh-colored cloth for the head and body, and black for the legs, so he didn't need to wear pants. One of the boys who hung around our house (and liked my pastries as well as he liked the girls) was discarding a striped shirt with a tear in it, which I easily mended. It looked fine for Ringo to wear. I had an old pair of pigskin driving gloves that had become permanently curled in the natural shape of relaxed fingers. Of course I knew that the reason he was called Ringo was because he wore a lot of rings on his fingers, so I bought several rings at the dime store, and sewed the rings onto the fingers of the stuffed gloves. I was having fun!

I had plenty of pictures to go by, to create a face on the head I had made with the cloth. I used flat buttons of blue for the famous blue eyes, and practiced on paper drawing the distinctive shape of the Ringo mouth.

I was really happy with how well he was shaping up, and longed to talk about it. But I was determined that he would be a total surprise on Christmas morning.

Finding time and place to work on him was hard: I was at my job all the hours the girls were at school. I was staying up quite late at night to create Ringo! As he came together more, there was the problem of keeping him hidden. No place in our house was safe. I kept the pieces in various bags and boxes in the trunk of my car, or in corners in my office at work. A few days before Christmas I found at the supermarket a big empty toilet-paper box for my car trunk. I sat Ringo down in it, brought his knees up to his chin and stuffed his feet and elbows down to the bottom of the box. All that showed at the top of the box were the wig, the be-ringed fingers, and the black knees. I closed the trunk.

When I did my last Christmas grocery shopping, the checkout boy was carrying my heavy bags out to my car for me. I unlocked the trunk and flung it open.

"Aaaaaaaa!" I thought the boy was about to drop everything and flee. (It did, certainly, look to be a dead body stuffed into my trunk!) I had to show him what it was, and he was fascinated.

Late that night the girls finally went to sleep. I brought Ringo out and sat him on the living-room couch by the Christmas tree. I arranged his arms and legs, and stepped back. He was lightweight, stuffed with rags, but he had a full sized man's body, and gave an amazing impression of a real man sitting there. It was gratifying to see how well he had turned out.

Early Christmas morning the girls were eager to rush into the living room to see what gifts there might be for them. I told them, "Someone special is coming this morning, so get nicely dressed." (I wanted to take pictures.) Louise said, "It's probably just one of Mom's boyfriends."

They did get dressed, while I went in to turn on the Christmas tree. In the dim light, it really seemed to be a live man sitting on our couch.

I spoke to him as they entered, "I want you to meet my daughter, Louise. And this is an ardent fan of yours, Elaine Miller."

Louise grabbed my arm. " Is it ..."

Elaine stood with hand to mouth. "It's ... it's ..." She took a few steps toward him.

"He's not real ... but he's ... he's Ringo!!" She lifted him up with delight, and danced with him, and hugged him, laughing and crying. Then both girls were dancing with him.

Louise exclaimed, "Oh Mom, did you <u>make</u> him?" I nodded, with happy tears of my own. I really did manage to give Elaine what she wanted. I gave her Ringo. What a joy.

Ringo was a member of the family the rest of that year. The girls could stand with him between them, one of his arms over the shoulder of each girl as they held him around his waist, then go strolling around the neighborhood. He looked so real that everyone would do a double take, then laugh and exclaim.

We sat him in the car wherever we went, and he attracted many double-takes. If I drove out alone at night, I would keep him beside me in the car and feel perfectly safe with my male escort.

One morning I took him to work before others arrived. I sat him in my office, in my own chair, with his hands folded on my desk, while I sat in another chair reading a report. It was fun when my secretary came in to see, "Who was that man sitting at Beth's desk?" Then the gasp, and the laugh. This was repeated by several colleagues, and then by our Director. Everyone enjoyed him.

I left him in another chair all day, because any visitor to our office was brought to see him. All recognized him as Ringo: the Beatle hair, and the rings on the hands did it.

Then the school year ended. Elaine prepared to fly back home to her family in Texas. She would no longer have a bedroom all her own, so needed to abandon some of her possessions. So … what about Ringo?

"Oh, he's coming with me. No way am I leaving him behind!" I tried to figure a way to pack him. But Elaine insisted he was travelling with her.

"If there's no empty seat, he can ride on my lap." Standing in line at the airport he attracted admiring attention. In the end, the airline didn't object to the "free passenger."

Back in Austin, as I heard it, Elaine's family and friends enjoyed Ringo for some years. Then when Elaine went to college, she left him at home. I heard that eventually her mother hung him on a clothes hanger in a closet. Years later, no one could remember, whatever happened to Ringo? Maybe he still turns up occasionally at some yard sale, or Salvation Army store.

I like to think that he might appear on the Antique Roadshow. As a piece of Beatle memorabilia, he could be a prime object.

For me, the life-size Ringo rag doll I created will always be a favorite memory. Also the memory of the fourteen-year-old girl, with clasped hands, exclaiming rapturously,

"All I want is Ringo!"

~ 21 ~
THE SOUTHERN EDGE

Today's news says that the Malaysian airline declares its plane is down in the south Indian Ocean, west of Perth, Australia, and all the people on board are lost. All of us have been following the story for days.

It recalls to me one sunset in 1975. I was standing on the huge beach at Yala, on the south shore of Sri Lanka, looking south over that same Indian Ocean (where the plane is now down). There were big waves, one after another, after another, relentlessly crashing. It was a very wide beach, edged with giant sand dunes, each as big as a house. Everything was on a huge scale.

I was feeling very very small. And insignificant. What I remember now is how aware I was, at that time, of the immensity of the distance that those waves had to come. Because there was no land from there, a few degrees north of the equator, all the way down through the southern hemisphere to Antarctica. Nothing but water, water, and more water. I felt that I was at the very edge of the world.

No wonder that, in 2014, the plane was given up for lost, in all that vast emptiness.

In 1975 Ann and Blake and I were spending three days in a bungalow, beside the lake that lies on the other side of those dunes. As I understood it, this lake was of scientific interest due to the variety of minerals that could be extracted there. Because of Ann's science connections, she had been able to arrange for us to stay in the bungalow used as a visitors' accommodation.

There was a wild animal preserve, called Yala, extending for thousands of acres, just east and north of the lake property. We had come to Yala to take a conducted tour to see the jungle. We were warned that there was no fencing of any sort between the lake property and the preserve, so the animals could (and did!) roam around the lake.

From our verandah we were pleased to have glimpsed, over there in the jungle, some antlered creatures, some slithering shapes (leopards were plentiful), and some monkeys swinging through the trees. We had been cautioned to be wary, and to be sure to stay inside the bungalow after dark. Yes indeed, we would.

Two youngish local men came, in response to our inquiries, to take us in their jeep for a half-day tour into the animal preserve. We doused ourselves with sunscreen and mosquito repellent (which had become a daily ritual). We dressed in light cotton clothing and wide hats, picked up binoculars, cameras, and canteens of water, and were off into the jungle. It was 5:30 in the morning. (Tropical people usually are active before dawn, and take rest in the afternoon heat.)

A jungle is a busy, noisy, colorful place. The vegetation is often extremely tall, and fiercely green. Probably banana trees are the only things we know that have leaves that are so large and so intensely green, as many tropical plants are. Flowers are a variety of vivid colors, as are many of the birds and butterflies. There are insects that hum and buzz and chirrup. We had chattering wanderoo monkeys overhead, and calling birds that we couldn't even see among the thick foliage. There was a particular kind of green pigeon with a plaintive whistle.

Shrieking peacocks, native here, strutted ardently around with fully fanned-out tails of magnificent radiant colors. The drab little female didn't look very impressed. How can she possibly choose, among all this glory?

We had squirrels, and mongoose. Large iguanas heavily wriggled their way along the ground. We saw some of the local spotted deer. A sambhur stag held high his regally antlered head.

In wet places there were native wild water buffalo. (Good to see them in their natural state, not pulling carts or laden with burdens for humans.) There were snowy egrets and black-necked ibis, and roseate spoonbills, and flamingos. I was overwhelmed!

"Oh look!" The driver stopped for us to watch, across a large clearing, a group of elephants of varying sizes.

"These are three females and their young," commented Ann, who is a biology teacher back home. "The Asian-elephant females don't have tusks. They are luckier than the African-elephant females, who do have tusks, and are hunted for their ivory just as the males are. Here only the males have ivory to be killed for. Maybe this elephant species is more likely to survive the human onslaught." I was enchanted to watch them feeding, and caressing their little ones, and rubbing against each other. Real elephants, doing real elephant things! Not just a film.

"We hope we can show you one of our tuskers," said the driver. "There is a mature male that is wandering in this area, and I think I heard him crashing around not far away." The driver was doing a good job of maneuvering the jeep around the thick undergrowth, often using tracks created by animals habitually passing through. (In this part of the world, elephants are famous for creating passages through the dense jungle, that humans were later happy to use as roads.)

"Oh yes. I hear him over there." Within minutes we could see, through the jungle tangle, the unmistakable big grey form. Yes, there is the snaking trunk, then the great flapping ears, the small bright eyes—and the white curve of tusk. All half-seen through the tangle of vines. We have found our tusker. Now he has turned to face us. He lifts his trunk. And he bellows! Instantly the driver is turning the steering wheel and backing the jeep. "Hold on!" he yells. He is backing and turning and backing and turning, and getting us out of that tangle as fast as he can. The three of us are holding on to each other as we lurch through the jungle.

The big elephant does not follow.

We have had a real adventure. What a day!

Our last day at Yala was when I had been standing on the beach looking south toward Antarctica, over the enormity of empty water. Musing on my insignificance.

Ann and Blake had joined me then, at the beach, and we had encountered a very handsome local youth, maybe 16 years old. He wore only a loincloth. We had full view of his well-toned muscular and graceful body. He had lustrous dark cocoa-colored skin, luxuriant wavy black hair, alert black eyes, and enticingly smiling full lips, a perfectly splendid specimen of young manhood of Sri Lanka.

His English was clear. He wanted to come to America. He asked us where we lived, and when I said, "California," he said, "Oh, you are a movie star."

I laughed. "No indeed. There are millions of people living in California who have nothing to do with the movies."

Blake was, in fact, a Canadian drama teacher, and was a skilled mime. He began to play around the beach, miming with the boy. Ann and I were photographing the beguiling lithe limbs and the charming laughing face. What a gorgeous boy. If any movie scout ever saw him, he probably would make it into films, Ann and I agreed.

The sun was being drawn into the ocean. The boy had disappeared down the beach. Blake warned, "We'd better get back before dark." He and Ann gathered their things.

I said, "I'll be right along." And they left.

Where we live in America, in temperate northern latitudes, the lag in time between sunset and dark is a long lovely interval. That dusky interval shortens as one travels south toward the equator. Right on the equator, that interval is very brief indeed; it grows dark almost immediately after sunset. And at the time I am describing, I was almost on the equator.

I had lingered to photograph the gorgeous sunset colors of sea and sky, and then had headed back the considerable distance to the bungalow. I had imprudently stayed photographing until the sun had gone down. Rapidly, night was falling!

Twice before, I had made the little hike, along the lake, from the bungalow to the gap in the dunes that led to the ocean beach. But I hadn't really paid attention to the distance, or to the time it took to walk. While I now hurry along the path, the glowing colors of lake and sky are rapidly darkening. Ah, there ahead I see the lighted window in the bungalow. Ann and Blake will be concerned. I am almost running when I see before me a log across the path. I don't remember that log being there. But I prepare to step up on it and on over, when … it <u>moves!</u> No log—it is a crocodile!

It scrambles and splashes into the lake, and hastily leaves. But not as fast as I do!!! My feet are <u>flying</u> as I flee back to the cottage and into the comforting arms of my friends. No, we didn't venture outside at night at all.

Now, four decades later, what a luxury it is to recall that time. How privileged I was, to be in that place. And to sense my insignificance.

Few places are left in this world where so large a swath of land has preserved this incredible diversity of life forms, the products of millions of years of biological evolution. Here were all these varieties of trees, shrubs, vines, herbs, grasses, mosses, with all these different shapes and sizes and colors, of leaves and flowers and seeds. All the different animals and birds and reptiles and insects, with all the different ways of walking, crawling, slithering, swimming, flying. Wearing different skin or fur or scales or feathers. Different ways of eating, sleeping, mating, nesting, socializing. Different kinds of eyes even have different ways of seeing! And <u>all</u> of it intermeshed, interacting!!!

As for me, at 93 years, I am surely reaching my end. How glorious that I had that Yala experience, however brief.

May Yala continue its evolution for more and more eons beyond me.

~ 22 ~
DREAM OF A JOURNEY

I dream that I am walking along a road. In the dream my legs are walking normally (not needing the walker that I need for every step I take now, at 92 years old). It is pleasant going at a leisurely pace, with other people walking in both directions. Some look familiar, but I walk alone on my own personal journey. I am wearing comfortable clothes, and carrying a small piece of luggage with some clothing and other things, to stay somewhere.

As I proceed I notice that I have lost my sun hat. Some time later, I have lost my jacket. I feel some concern, but decide it's all right, I don't really need them. I go on undismayed.

It isn't clear where I am going, or for what purpose, but there is no doubt at all that I am proceeding, and I am perfectly comfortable with that. I stop to eat and drink with other acquaintances.

I take up my solitary walk, and then I notice that I have lost my light baggage. I am somewhat disturbed that I have no fresh clothes to change into. The long cotton skirt and sleeveless top I am wearing are beginning to look rumpled. I decide it really doesn't matter.

I go on contentedly. The journey is essential, and it is pleasant.

Uh oh! I find I have lost my purse. I look around with concern. I'll have no money. And not even a credit card. Won't I need money to get checked in? What is it that I'm to get "checked in" to? I can't remember. But again, I feel that I need have no anxiety.

I calm my mind, and continue to walk along. I never seem to wonder about direction or anything. I just proceed, and everything is fine.

What about my I.D.? I have no I.D. Surely I am going to need to have I.D. somewhere ahead. Again, as each time before, I'm sure that I need not be dismayed. Where I am going, I don't need to "have" anything. I am just me, and I am complete as I am.

~~~~~

I woke up feeling cozy and comfortable in my bed. It was just dawn light of a sweet day. Oh. I lost my purse, didn't I? Then I see it, right over there. It's not lost. I have my I.D. I feel safe. To live in this world, I do need my I.D.

~~~~~

I love this dream. I feel it is about the end of life. It is all easy and uncomplicated.

I don't need anything, not even I.D.

THE END

ACKNOWLEDGEMENTS

My daughter, Shakti Gawain, has supported me and lovingly encouraged me to write and publish my stories. Her confidence in my ability is a mainstay.

Gina Vucci helped me get my stories together into a book, and returned to me again and again as I strugglingly tried and tried to learn to use the computer. I thank her.

Thomas Centolella's class in Creative Writing has given me the reason for actually writing two pages of these stories nearly every week. His comments and suggestions have been unfailingly welcome and helpful, as have the critiques of my classmates. Tom encouraged me to aspire to a better level of literary excellence, while having fun remembering, and sharing, details of events scattered throughout my long life. I am grateful.

Thanks to Mary Hammond, who came to help me to organize and to proofread all the stories, and who encouraged me to believe in the reality of the book.

Then Amy Metzenbaum transformed my world. Together with Jo Anne Smith, they provided the vital research and mechanics, and personal encouragement, needed to get this publication done. I am immensely grateful.

Without all this friendly loving help, it never would have happened.

Lastly, I want to acknowledge the friends and family who peopled these stories as companions in my life adventures, and whose names you will discover herein.

Made in the USA
San Bernardino, CA
02 September 2015